A Hist[illegible] York[illegible] People, [illegible]jects & Places

Paul Chrystal

DestinWorld publishing

'York is, of course, the guide-book man's paradise, and not without good reason, for if you want the past, here it is weighing tons.'

- J.B. Priestley, English Journey (1933)

'Beware how you destroy your antiquities, guard them with religious care! They are what give you a decided character and superiority over other provincial cities. You have lost much, take care of what remains.'

- William Etty 1787–1849

'The history of York is the history of England.'

- George VI, when Duke of York, 1920

First Edition 2023

ISBN 978 1 7398194 2 2

British Library Cataloguing-in-Publication Data

A catalogue record for this book is available from the British Library.

Published by Destinworld Publishing Ltd.

www.destinworld.com

Printed in the United Kingdom

FSC
www.fsc.org
MIX
Paper from responsible sources
FSC® C014540

A History of York in 101 People, Objects & Places

Paul Chrystal

About the author

Paul Chrystal was educated at the universities of Hull and Southampton, where he took degrees in classics and then, for the next 35 years, worked in medical publishing, much of the time as an international sales director for one market or another, and creating medical education programmes for global pharmaceutical companies.

More recently, he has been history advisor to local visitor attractions including the National Trust (Goddards) and York's Chocolate Story, writing features for national newspapers.

He is the author of numerous books on a wide range of subjects, including social and industrial history, and many local histories on York, and Yorkshire towns and cities.

See: www.paulchrystal.com

Acknowledgements

Thanks to Ruth Ogden, Deputy Librarian, St John's College, Oxford and the President and Fellows of St John Baptist College, Oxford, for allowing me to use the images of the Holy Trinity Bestiary. To York Archaeological Trust for the image of the Mansion House dead cat, and to Tim Barber, Real Yorkshire Tours, for giving permission to use his superb photography from the Treasurer's House, viewable at www.realyorkshireblog.com/post/the-treasurers-house-york-frank-green-s-palace-of-entertainment. The Printer's Devil photograph comes courtesy of Visit York, © Jim Richardson; thanks to Sarah Foster, Communications Manager.

Every effort has been made to source copyright holders but where this has not been possible we will be happy to acknowledge and credit in reprints or new editions.

By the same author

York Through the Lens of 'The Press' (2022)

The History of Britain in 100 Objects (2022)

The Making of Roman York (2022)

The Rowntrees: The Early History (2021)

A Historical Guide to Roman York (2021)

Life in York 100 Years Ago (The exclusive Hanstock Collection, YAYAS), 2021

York: A Rare Insight (The exclusive Evelyn Collection, YAYAS), (2020)

Old York (2019)

Pubs in and Around York (2018)

Contents

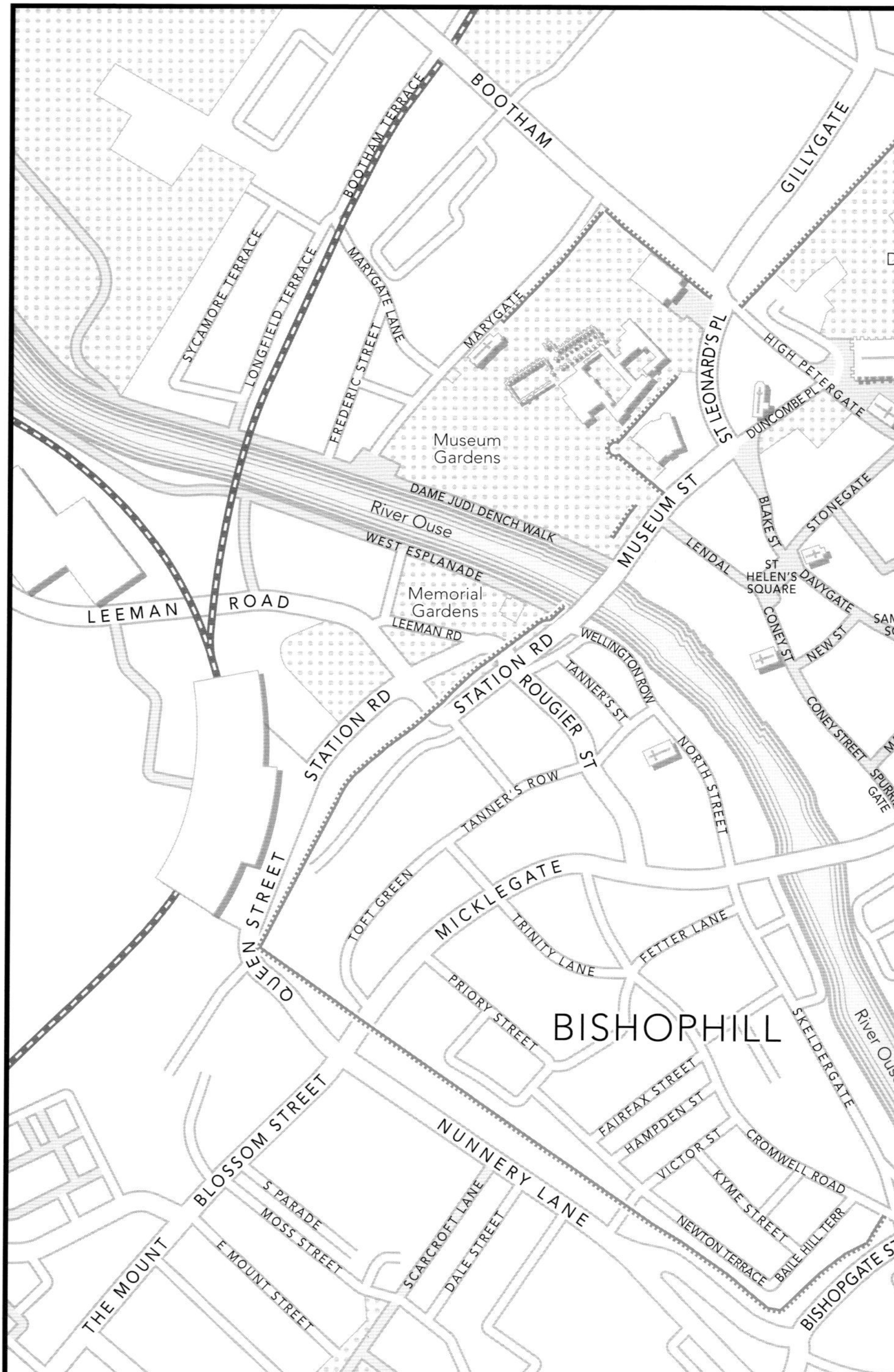

BOOTHAM
GILLYGATE
BOOTHAM TERRACE
SYCAMORE TERRACE
LONGFIELD TERRACE
MARYGATE LANE
FREDERIC STREET
MARYGATE
ST LEONARD'S PL
HIGH PETERGATE
DUNCOMBE PL
Museum Gardens
DAME JUDI DENCH WALK
River Ouse
WEST ESPLANADE
MUSEUM ST
LENDAL
BLAKE ST
STONEGATE
ST HELEN'S SQUARE
DAVYGATE
Memorial Gardens
LEEMAN ROAD
LEEMAN RD
STATION RD
STATION RD
WELLINGTON ROW
TANNER'S ST
ROUGIER ST
CONEY ST
NEW ST
CONEY STREET
NORTH STREET
TANNER'S ROW
MICKLEGATE
TOFT GREEN
TRINITY LANE
FETTER LANE
QUEEN STREET
PRIORY STREET
BISHOPHILL
SKELDERGATE
FAIRFAX STREET
HAMPDEN ST
VICTOR ST
CROMWELL ROAD
KYME STREET
NEWTON TERRACE
BAILE HILL TERR
BLOSSOM STREET
NUNNERY LANE
S PARADE
MOSS STREET
E MOUNT STREET
SCARCROFT LANE
DALE STREET
THE MOUNT

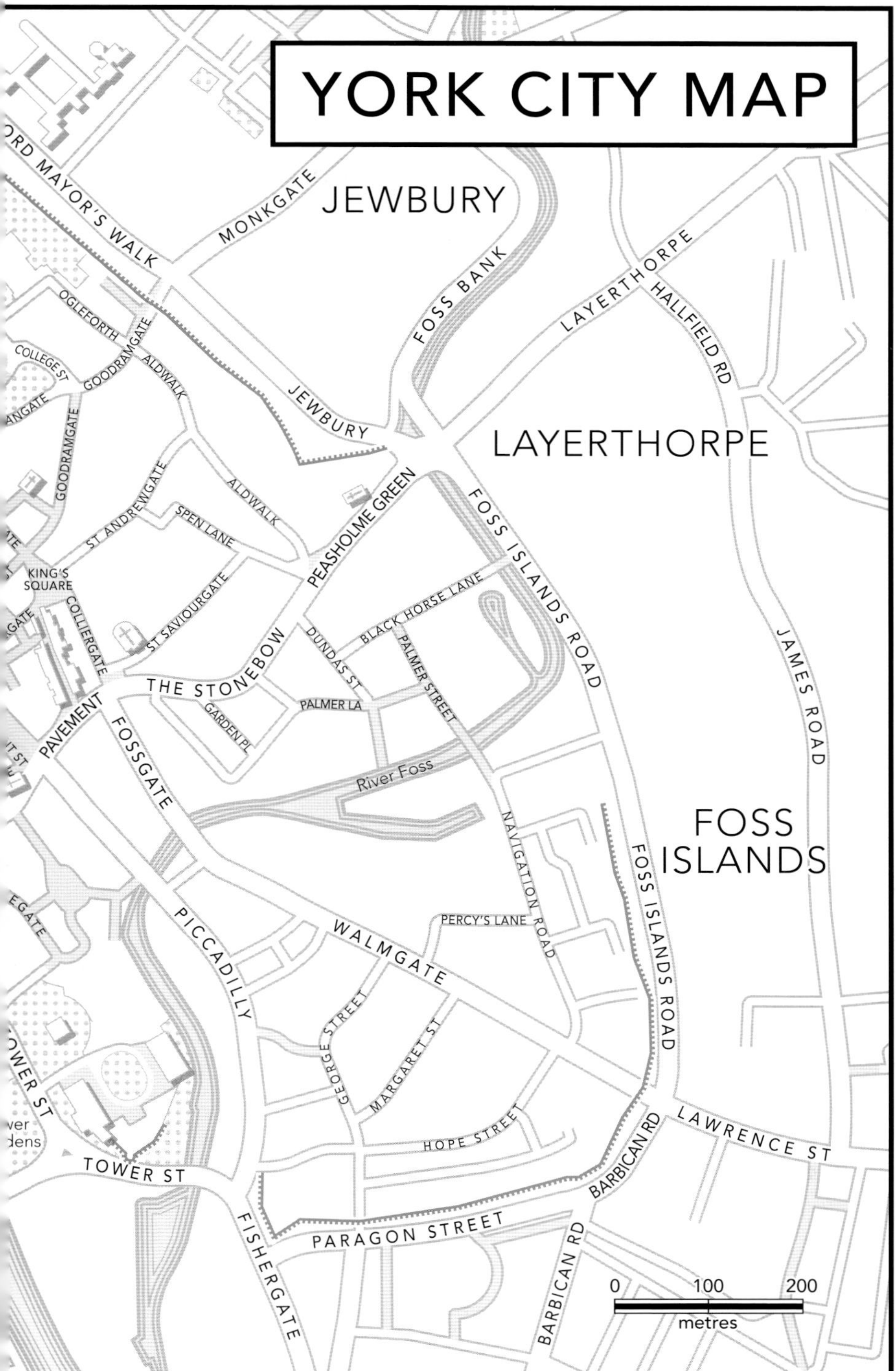
YORK CITY MAP
JEWBURY
LAYERTHORPE
FOSS ISLANDS
LORD MAYOR'S WALK
MONKGATE
FOSS BANK
LAYERTHORPE
HALLFIELD RD
OGLEFORTH
COLLEGE ST
GOODRAMGATE
ALDWALK
JEWBURY
PEASHOLME GREEN
FOSS ISLANDS ROAD
ST ANDREWGATE
SPEN LANE
KING'S SQUARE
COLLIERGATE
ST SAVIOURGATE
BLACK HORSE LANE
DUNDAS ST
PALMER STREET
JAMES ROAD
THE STONEBOW
GARDEN PL
PALMER LA
PAVEMENT
FOSSGATE
River Foss
NAVIGATION ROAD
PICCADILLY
PERCY'S LANE
WALMGATE
GEORGE STREET
MARGARET ST
HOPE STREET
LAWRENCE ST
BARBICAN RD
TOWER ST
PARAGON STREET
FISHERGATE
0
100
200
metres

Introduction

This book is an accessible and eminently dippable history of York as shown by 101 significant objects, people and places. They are presented in no particular order, neither chronological nor by location, so as if to offer the reader a varied and random reading experience – just as if you are ambling at a leisurely pace along the city's gates (streets), through the bars (gates) and in and out the snickelways (alleys), coming across this, that or the other purely by pleasant chance in what can be your personal journey of serendipity.

With only 101 objects, people and places, the book can have no claim to being comprehensive – York has so much to offer. Instead, it features a large number of the less obvious, more surprising things, people and places connected with York, rather than yet another rehash of Dick Turpin, Guido Fawkes, the myriad ghosts, the Shambles and so on.

So you will hear about the poet Shelley – one of the few visitors underwhelmed by the majesty of the Minster, about crazy George Frederick Sitwell of the outrageous Sitwell family who ended his days in the York Lunatic Asylum, about the bizarre (to say the very least) marriage of Arthur Munby and Hannah Cullwick, and that Viking beserker, Ivar the Boneless; you will read about 'The Phoenix' and the immutable Black Babies, The Mansion House and its Edgar Allen Poe-like dead cat, and about a woman sold in Pavement for a few bob; we will regale you with doom knockers, doom windows and doom stones; with the Sigismund sword and with Captain Tom Moore's funeral sword; with exploding bananas and with racism in the Rowntree family.

So, this is a book that will give you a different, more unconventional view of York, very much in keeping with a city that is freighted with history.

Cover image: 'The York Globe' by Ben Staves. Courtesy of and ©Ben Staves. Staves Art www.stavesart.com @stavesart

1

The White Heather Club

England's first women's cricket club

Cricket Match Played by the Countess of Derby and Other Ladies, 1779', Marylebone Cricket Club; in the Tate Gallery (T03031).

Today, women's cricket is thriving – the only surprising thing about that is why it has taken so long. As with football, it probably has something to do with men and their insecurity relating to male bastions in sport.

England's first women's cricket club, the White Heather Club, was formed in 1887 at Nun Appleton near York by 'eight ladies, all from wealthy families and mostly members of the aristocracy' (Paul Salway, *A Novel Match at Cricket*). For most women of the day, kitting yourself out was prohibitively expensive, but the club expanded, and, to quote Tessa McLaren of Wisden, it mostly comprised of 'Yorkshire ladies with enough money to pay their own expenses'. In other words, women's cricket in England was the preserve of the upper strata of society until the formation of Women's Cricket Association in 1926. Once that happened, women's cricket in England gained popularity across the wider population. Nevertheless, the White Heather Club survived until 1957.

The first reported game appeared in The *Reading Mercury* on 26 July 1745 of a match that took place between the villages of Bramley and

Hambledon near Guildford in Surrey:

> *The greatest cricket match that was played in this part of England was... between eleven maids of Bramley and eleven maids of Hambledon, all dressed in white. The Bramley maids had blue ribbons and the Hambledon maids red ribbons on their heads. The Bramley girls got 119 notches and the Hambledon girls 127. There was of bothe sexes the greatest number that ever was seen on such an occasion. The girls bowled, batted, ran and catched as well as most men could do in that game.*

Reading this quaint piece, one wonders whether virginity was considered a prerequisite for participation. By 1890 two professional teams imaginatively called The Reds and The Blues travelled the length and breadth of England to play local sides, just like William Clarke's All-England XI from a few decades earlier. Known as the 'Original English Lady Cricketers', they were paid six pence a day playing in exhibition matches to large crowds. The team was highly successful until its manager absconded with the profits, forcing the women to disband the team.

In 1926 the Women's Cricket Association was founded, and in 1934–35 sent a team to Australia and New Zealand, playing the first Women's Test match between England and Australia in December 1934. Australia repaid the visit in 1937, and, since World War Two, tours have gone from strength to strength. The International Women's Cricket Council was formed in 1958 by Australia, England, the Netherlands, New Zealand and South Africa; India, Denmark and several West Indian islands joined later. A women's World Cup was established in 1973, two years before the men, and England and Australia played in the first women's matches at Lord's in 1976.

England Women will play their first ever Test Match at Lord's, the ECB confirms - but not until 2026! This comes hot on the heels of the late June 2023 report in which the ECB recognises need for significant reform in English criscket which was found to suffer from "widespread and deep-rooted" racism, sexism, elitism and class-based discrimination at all levels of the game.

The 317-page report from the Independent Commission for Equity in Cricket (Icec), drew on evidence from more than 4,000 players, coaches, administrators and fans. The general attitude adopted by many men was, and is, based on ignorance, believing that cricket, as W.G. Grace pronounced, 'not a game for women, and although the fair sex occasionally join in a picnic game, they are not constitutionally adapted for the sport!'

See:

Duncan, Isabelle (2013). *Skirting the Boundary: A History of Women's Cricket. London: The Robson Press.*

Nicholson, Rafaelle (2019). *Ladies and Lords: A History of Women's Cricket in Britain. Oxford: Peter Lang.*

Velija, Philippa (2015). *Women's Cricket and Global Processes: The Emergence and Development of Women's Cricket as a Global Game. Basingstoke.*

2

The Richard III Museum at Monk Bar

Take part in the trial of Richard III

The famous late-16th-century portrait of Richard III was on loan to the Yorkshire Museum in York in 2021. It has been loaned by the National Portrait Gallery as part of its nationwide Coming Home project, in which the gallery sends portraits of iconic individuals to places they are closely associated with.

This fascinating museum is housed in Monk Bar, at the top of the steps leading up to the city walls at the end, or beginning, of Goodramgate depending on which way you are looking. The museum opened in 1992 in a successful attempt by creator Michael S.

Bennett, a former York tour guide, to set the historical record of Yorkist York straight over this much-maligned monarch. An important part of the museum is devoted to a special exhibit called 'The Trial of Richard III', where you can hear the evidence, both for and against, and decide for yourself if the king in the dock actually did kill his nephews, the unfortunate 'Princes in the Tower'. You can also relive the controversy through mock mediaeval tabloid newspapers.

Monk Bar

Built around 1330, it was originally called Monkgate Bar. At 63ft, it is the tallest of York's Bars. Designed as a self-contained fortress, assailants had to cross each floor to reach the next flight of stairs, thus exposing themselves to defensive fire. A perfect fortress, the Bar features loopholes (for bows and arrows); gun ports and murder holes from which heavy objects and boiling water might be dropped. The coat of arms is Plantagenet. The Bar was used as a prison in the 16th century for recusant Catholics, and others. In 1588 Robert Walls was imprisoned for 'drawing blood in a fray'. The barbican was removed in the early 1800s. To rent the rooms at the top, one Thomas Pak (Master Mason at the Minster) paid 4s per annum.

Little Ease

A tiny prison cell in Monk Bar, little over five feet in diameter. In 1594 Alice Bowman, a local recusant, was held here. Bowman was accused of conspiring to steal the severed heads of Catholic rebels from Ouse Bridge, where they were displayed as a warning to Catholic sympathisers. From 1845 to 1913, a police inspector lived there.

See:

Drewett, Richard; 1984. *The Trial of Richard III.* Stroud.

England, Barbara, ed., 1986. *Richard III and the North of England.* University of Hull.

"York Minster says Richard III should be buried in Leicester". *BBC News.* London. 7 February 2013.

3

Beilby Porteus

One of the 'forgotten abolitionists'

The Court of Death (1820) was based on Anglican Bishop Beilby Porteus's poem from 1772, Death: A Poetical Essay. The figures in the monumental painting were life-size. Death is surrounded by personifications, including Despair, Fever, Consumption, Hypochondria, Apoplexy, Gout, Dropsy, Suicide, Delirium Tremens, Intemperance, Remorse, Pleasure, Pestilence, Famine, War, and Conflagration. To the right, a warrior, an orphaned infant, and a widow show some of the people afflicted. In the foreground, Old Age is supported by Faith (Detroit Institute of Arts).

Born in York, Beilby Porteus (1731–1809) was the youngest but one of 19 children. Beilby's parents were Virginian planters who had returned to England in 1720. Educated at York and at Ripon Grammar School, he was a Classics scholar at Christ's College, Cambridge, becoming a fellow in 1752. In 1759 he won the Seatonian Prize for his poem Death: A Poetical Essay, a work for which he is still remembered. Porteus became Bishop of Chester and then London.

He was an active and vigorous campaigner against slavery, criticising the Church's apathy regarding, for example, the plight of 350 black slaves in its Codrington Estates in Barbados in his The Civilisation, Improvement and Conversion of the Negroe Slaves in the British West-India Islands Recommended. This was one of the first challenges to the establishment in an eventual 26-year campaign to eradicate slavery in the British West Indian colonies. Porteus made a huge contribution and eventually turned to other means of achieving his aims, including writing, encouraging political initiatives, and supporting the sending of mission workers to Barbados and Jamaica. Deeply concerned about the lives of the slaves as a result of the reports he received, Porteus became a committed and passionate abolitionist.

Beilby Porteus is one of the most significant, under-rated church figures of the 18th century. His sermons were read by many, and his legacy as a foremost abolitionist was such that his name was almost as well known in the early 19th century as those of Wilberforce and Thomas Clarkson – but 100 years later he had become one of the 'forgotten abolitionists', and today his role has largely been ignored and his name has been consigned to the footnotes of history.

Porteus's most lasting contribution was one for which he is little-known, the Sunday Observance Act of 1781, which legislated how the public was allowed to spend their recreation time at weekends for the following 200 years, until the passage of the Sunday Trading Act of 1994.

See:

McKelvie, Graham. *The Development of Official Anglican Interest in World Mission 1783–1809: With Special Reference to Bishop Beilby Porteus,* PhD diss. (U. Aberdeen, 1984)

Tennant, Bob. 'Sentiment, Politics, and Empire: A Study of Beilby Porteus's Antislavery Sermon', in *Discourses of Slavery and Abolition: Britain and its Colonies, 1760–1838*, ed Brycchan Carey, Markman Ellis, Basingstoke, 2004.

4

Sir Thomas Herbert and Charles I's Execution Vest, 1649

The bloody vest of Charles I (photograph courtesy of the Museum of London).

Seven years of internecine civil war claimed the lives of thousands, including the King of England himself. Tuesday, 30 January 1649 was Charles I's last day on earth. After years of fractious political and military conflicts between the royalists and the Parliamentarians during the English Civil War, England's king was arrested and tried on Saturday, 27 January. The Parliamentarian High Court of Justice declared Charles was guilty of attempting to 'uphold in himself an unlimited and tyrannical power to rule according to his will, and to overthrow the rights and liberties of the people'. Treason. Accordingly, he was sentenced to death.

The king's final two days were spent in St James's Palace, surrounded by his most loyal subjects and his family. Charles spent much of the day before his execution day praying with the Bishop of London, William Juxon. That same day he burnt his personal papers and correspondence.

On 30 January, Charles rose early and began dressing at 5am in fine clothes, all black, and a blue sash. He instructed the Gentleman of his Bedchamber, Thomas Herbert, how to dispose of the few possessions he had left. He requested one extra shirt from Herbert, so that the crowd would not see him shiver from the cold and attribute it to cowardice.

Charles came through the window of the banqueting hall to the scaffold in what Herbert described as 'the saddest sight England ever saw'.

Sir Thomas Herbert, 1st Baronet (1606–1682), was born in York in a house now known as the Herbert House on Pavement. Between 1626 and 1629 he travelled with the Earl of Pembroke on a tour that took in a visit to the Shah of Persia, who gifted him a Persian costume and a black page boy. Herbert started as a Parliamentarian but in 1647 converted to the king's cause, becoming personal assistant to Charles I. In 1678 Herbert published Threnodia Carolina, an account of the last two years of the king's life. He tells how he was too distraught to be with the king on the scaffold and burst into tears when the king seemed upset by some news he had brought.

At the restoration of the monarchy in 1660 Herbert returned to London having been offered a general pardon. After this Herbert dropped out of public life, but remained in London in York Street, Westminster, until the Great Plague in 1666, when he retired to York. He died at Petergate House on 1 March 1682, and was buried in the church of St Crux, where his widow placed a brass tablet in his memory. There is a blue plaque on High Petergate outside his house at number 11.

See:

'Sir Thomas Herbert's House, Pavement'. York Conservation Trust.

An Inventory of the Historical Monuments in City of York, Volume 5, Central. London: HMSO. 1981.

'Thomas Herbert (1606-1682)'. York Civic Trust.

Historic England, '11 Lady Peckitts Yard (1257535). National Heritage List for England.

5

Henrietta Eliza Vaughan Stannard

'The author to whom we owe the most finished and faithful rendering ever yet given of the character of the British soldier.' John Ruskin

Henrietta Stannard went by three additional names: her maiden name of Palmer, Violet Whyte and John Strange Winter.

Promotional poster for Private Tinker, a novel by John Strange Winter (a pen name of Henrietta Eliza Vaughan Stannard).

Born in The Cottage, Trinity Lane, she was the only daughter of Henry Vaughan Palmer (d. 1877), rector of St Margaret's, York. Stannard (1856-1911) attended Bootham House School, after which, in 1874, she assumed the nom de plume Violet Whyte, writing for the Family Herald. In 1881 she published Cavalry Life, a collection of regimental sketches, in 1883, Regimental Legends and in 1885, Bootles Baby under the pseudonym of John Strange Winter, a character in one of her stories. Her (male) publisher refused to bring out the books under a feminine pseudonym, while the public assumed the author was a cavalry officer. All in all, she published about 100 novels and ten other books, as well as articles for the Cornhill and Temple Bar.

She married ex-soldier Arthur Stannard at Fulford, York, in 1884. In 1885 Bootle's Baby: A Story of the Scarlet Lancers was published in the Graphic selling two million copies in ten years. Between 1891 and 1895 she published her own weekly magazine and wrote Confessions of a Publisher in 1892, mocking patronising male publishers of the day. John Ruskin described John Strange Winter as 'the author to whom we owe the most finished and faithful rendering ever yet given of the character of the British soldier'. She was first president of the Writers' Club (1892), was a Fellow of the Royal Society of Literature and was president of the Society of Women Journalists from 1901 to 1903.

For a list of works, see:

http://www.victorianresearch.org/atcl/show_author.php?aid=758

See:

Lee, Elizabeth (1912), 'Stannard, Henrietta Eliza Vaughan'. Dictionary of National Biography (2nd supplement). London: Smith, Elder & Co.

6

John Moore

York's one and only black freeman

The Gild of Freemen of York processioning, in 2017, along Goodramgate to their annual church service, with the York Guard and York Waits leading the way. Courtesy of York Press.

In the later 17th century Moore, a native Moor, was the only black man on York's Freemen's Rolls – bluntly, albeit accurately, listed as John Moore – 'blacke'. Moore paid two amounts – 20 nobles (equivalent to 13s 6d) to the Common Chamber of the City of York and £4 to the city council – for this privilege in 1687. This permitted him to enjoy all the privileges of the freedom of the city: he could bear arms, he had the right to fish in the city's rivers and, since freemen were beneficial owners of the meadows, he could graze his animals on them.

> The Freemen's Roll of the city of York records, in October 1687: 'Ordered that John Moore the Blackmoore be Admitted to the Freedom of this Citty - paying twenty Nobles to the Common Chamber of this Citty. And it is left to my Lord Mayor's discretion to retorne him back what he pleases.'

See:

https://www.africansinyorkshireproject.com/british-black-presence-part-three.html

7

An Indifferent Shelley and Thomas Jefferson Hogg

'There was no end of pretty girls of all ranks to be found in the streets'

Joseph Severn's portrait of Percy Bysshe Shelley. The radical 19th century poet practised the politics of the plate. For Shelley and other liberals of his day, keeping sugar out of tea was a political statement against slavery.

Thomas Jefferson Hogg (1792 – 1862) was a barrister and friend of Percy Bysshe Shelley, whom he met at University College, Oxford, when they were both sent down on account of their avowed atheism as expressed in their work The Necessity of Atheism.

Both were advocates of free love and free thinking. Hogg then moved to York on a legal apprenticeship in spring 1812. He is probably best known for his The Life of Percy Bysshe Shelley, an unfinished biography of the poet.

Shelley's plan to visit Hogg in York was derailed when he fell in love with Harriet Westbrook, whom he married in Edinburgh, despite being firmly anti-marriage; Hogg, meanwhile, was showing an unhealthy interest in Harriet, which she rebuffed. Shelley did get to see Hogg in York; when he wasn't flirting with Harriet, Hogg was showing the newlyweds the city: 'York, in fact, is not a dull place… there is much, pleasant, cheerful society, much gentle hospitality… we had races twice, there were assizes.' Hogg was most impressed by 'the superb Minster, a permanent gratification of which one can never tire; and the musical performances are well performed there.' Perhaps most typical of Hogg was his observation that 'there was no end of pretty girls of all ranks to be found in the streets, for the ancient city was always celebrated as an abode of beauty.' An agonising Hogg adds, 'it was at once pleasing and painful to meet them: delightful and dangerous.'

Try as he may, though, he could not persuade Shelley of York's reputation as a 'bower of beauty'. York 'disenchanted him'. No lover of art or architecture at the time, Shelley was decidedly underwhelmed by York Minster, which he 'viewed with indifference'.

'I took him into York Minster several times, but to no purpose; it was thrown away, entirely lost upon him.'

See:

David Palliser, *York as they saw it – from Alcuin to Lord Esher*, York, 1979.

Richard Holmes, *Shelley: The Pursuit,* London, 2005.

8

William Peckitt

Opening a window on the world

The wonderful Peckitt window crafted by his widow, Mary Peckitt.

William Peckitt was born in Husthwaite in 1731 and was one of England's foremost glass painters and stain glass makers. In fact, he is widely regarded as the most prominent and prolific glazier of his day and, according to the Oxford Dictionary of National Biography, was responsible for keeping the craft alive in the 18th century. Actually, 'it was William Peckitt who did most of the stained glass and painted glass work that survives from the second half of the eighteenth century.' (Cowen, 1985)

Patrons included the Dean of York and Horace Walpole, with commissions at New College, Oxford, and the cathedrals at Exeter, Lincoln and Ripon. The family moved to York in around 1750, where William worked in his father's glove-making business before setting himself up as a glass painter in Colliergate. He died in 1795 and is buried in St Martin-cum-Gregory, where Mary, his wife and assistant, made a stunning memorial window to him. His Commission Book is the earliest surviving account of glass painting and includes 315 works ranging from sash windows to cathedral windows.

In York, Peckitt's work can be seen at:

- York Minster – several windows including Abraham and Solomon in the south Transept. He carried out the resetting of, and repair to, the mediaeval glass throughout his life and painted the central sunburst motif to the Rose window in the South Transept.
- York, St Martin-cum-Gregory – the memorial window to his daughters.
- York City Art Gallery has several examples of his work.

St Martin-cum-Gregory, Micklegate and the Stained Glass Centre

Now redundant as a place of worship, but home to the superb Stained Glass Centre since 2008, this was established by the Stained Glass Trust, with the aim of encouraging the study and appreciation of stained glass, as well as breathing life back into St Martin-cum-Gregory. York has 60 per cent of the surviving in-situ mediaeval glass in the country, so it is particularly apt that this cutting-edge centre of excellence thrives in York. Moreover, William Peckitt (1731-1795), one of England's foremost church glaziers, was a local man and has windows dedicated to him in the church. Peckitt, his wife Mary, and Henry Gyles (1645–1709), three of the nation's leading lights in stained glass, are all, aptly, buried here.

The website gives us the mission statement:

- The Stained Glass Centre is a national resource for the discovery and interpretation of stained glass.
- Visitors participate in, and learn about, craft-skills, arts and industries that continue to play a vital role in the life of the city and region.
- Practitioners from all over the UK now have a national centre of excellence for the study and development of their craft.

Aged 62;
in the Chancel.
and Executed by
1796.

- People of all ages have the opportunity to learn about the historic importance of this beautiful art form as well as helping it to develop and flourish in the 21st century.
- The creation of the Stained Glass Centre in the former church of St Martin-cum-Gregory will give new life to one of York's most beautiful 'lost' buildings.

Harry Harvey (1922–2011)

Another leading light in York's celebrated history of stained-glass window design was Harry Harvey, who came to York in 1947 as assistant to Harry Stammers at the York School of Glass Painting. Working eventually from his own studio, Stammers completed in excess of 220 windows, the most famous being the glorious colourful window in the

Harry Harvey's maker's mark, St Martin in the Bull Ring, south chapel east window.

restored Guildhall in 1960. Over 70 Yorkshire churches are graced with his windows and he is also responsible for the Astronomical Clock in York Minster.

See:

Chrystal, Paul, *York's Churches & Places of Worship*, Catrine, 2016.

Cowen, Painton, *A Guide to Stained Glass in Britain,* London,1985.

9

York Minster Stoneyard

York Minster has something in common with the Forth Bridge – there is no end to the work needed on conservation and the restoration is never finished.

Here you can see two of the more interesting pieces awaiting installation. Note the frog emerging from the mouth of the creature on the left.

Alex McCallion, York Minster's Director of Works and Precinct, tells us that, 'Every stone replaced on the Minster is hand carved by our team of 15 masons and we have a rolling programme of conservation works needed to maintain the building for the next 30 years. Our current project, to conserve and restore the cathedral's 14th-century South Quire Aisle, involves repairing and replacing stone in 15 window bays and will take 11 years and £11m to complete.'

The website, https://yorkminster.org/discover/stories/story/centuries-of-expert-craftsmanship/, informs us that:

The yard moved to its current location in Deangate in 1913, where the Minster's team of 16 masons is now based. Today, York Minster is one of nine cathedrals in the country to maintain a permanent masons' workshop, with the team working up to 50 tonnes of stone each year as part of ongoing conservation projects.

Mason's marks

Each mason has their own unique and individual 'mason's mark' – a symbol carved into each stone they finish to identify who carved it. In the past, they were used to indicate that a piece of work was finished so that the mason could be paid. Mason's marks have been found on stones in parts of the Minster dating as far back as 1154. The same mason's marks used by craftsmen working on the Minster have also been found on other local churches, showing they used to travel from building to building for work.

10

Anne Brontë

'If finite power can do this, what is the ...'

Detail (Anne) from The Brontë Sisters (Anne Brontë; Emily Brontë; Charlotte Brontë), 1834, by Patrick Branwell Brontë (died 1848). National Portrait Gallery NPG 1725.

What was life like for the Brontë sisters? We learn from Christine Alexander in the Oxford Dictionary of National Biography that:

'Unlike many middle-class Victorian households, there was little censorship of reading in the Brontë parsonage. The Bible was staple fare; yet Patrick Brontë also encouraged an eclectic diet of Homer, Virgil, Shakespeare, Bunyan, Milton, Pope, Johnson, Gibbon, Cowper, Burns, Wordsworth, Coleridge, Scott, Southey and Byron …'

However, despite their father's best efforts to maximise educational opportunities for the surviving girls, they were always going to be constricted by the societal norms that dictated the course of middle-class women's lives: their only options were marriage, or careers as school mistress or governess. Of the three, only Emily never became a governess; she had a short spell teaching in Miss Patchett's school at Law Hill between Haworth and Halifax. Charlotte had teaching positions at Miss Margaret Wooler's school, and in Brussels with the Hegers. She became governess to the Sidgwicks, the Stonegappes, and the Lotherdales, then with Mrs White, at Upperhouse House, Rawdon, on 1841. Anne (1820–49) worked as governess for Mrs Ingham at Blake Hall, Mirfield, in 1839, then for Mrs Robinson at Thorp Green Hall, Little Ouseburn, near York.

Branwell, Anne's famously sybaritic brother, had aspirations to become an artist, but his attempts to succeed just led to a prodigal trip to London with Branwell in 1841 carousing in various dens of iniquity, while Anne attempted to keep him on the straight and narrow by finding work for him in January 1843, at Thorp Green Hall, where he was tutor to the Reverend Edmund Robinson's son living in the Monk's Lodge; this arrangement ended after three years when Branwell was dismissed. There is still controversy over why, but it seems likely that it involved Mrs Lydia Robinson and the two-year affair she conducted with Bramwell. Over 100 years later the lyrics to Simon and Garfunkel's *Mrs Robinson resonate: It's a little secret, just the Robinsons' affair. Most of all, you've got to hide it from the kids.* Indeed, Lydia Robinson was the inspiration behind the name of the character Mrs Robinson, who has an affair with an intelligent but confused young man, in Charles Webb's novel The Graduate (1963) and the 1967 film of the same name. Back in the 19th century, Elizabeth Gaskell wrote to her publisher describing Mrs Robinson as 'that bad woman who corrupted Branwell Brontë'.

The affair gave Anne no option but to quit the post she had held for over five years, leading her to reflect that 'during my stay I have had some very unpleasant and undreamt-of experiences of human nature.'

Before all this, however, Anne enjoyed her many visits to nearby York where she was particularly taken by the Minster. By May 1849 Anne was dying of tuberculosis, and about to make her final journal to

Scarborough, where she is buried. This also gave her one last chance to see York, and she, Charlotte Brontë and Ellen Nussey arrived there on 24 May. They stayed at the George Hotel on Coney Street.

They did some shopping to buy the clothes they would need for Scarborough. By then too weak to walk very far, Charlotte pushed her to the Minster in a hired bath chair. Anne gazed up silently and lovingly at the magnificent surroundings. She whispered one half-finished sentence: 'If finite power can do this, what is the …' before Charlotte wheeled her back to the hotel, worried that this rush of emotions might finish her sister off forever. It was clear what Anne was thinking – if weak man's powers can create something so magnificent, how magnificent will be the creation of God be that I am soon to see?

Ellen Nussey wrote a short description of these days for Elizabeth Gaskell, *A Short Account Of The Last Days Of Dear A.B:*

> *By her request we went to the Minster, and to her it was an overpowering pleasure; not for its own imposing and impressive grandeur only, but because it brought to her susceptible nature a vital and overwhelming sense of omnipotence. She said, while gazing at the structure, 'If finite power can do this, what is the…?' and here emotion stayed her speech, and she was hastened to a less exciting scene.*

Anne Brontë died on 28 May 1849 in Scarborough.

See:

Charlesworth, Chris 'Bridge Over Troubled Water'. *The Complete Guide to the Music of Paul Simon and Simon & Garfunkel.* Omnibus Press, 1997.

Chrystal, Paul, *Haworth Timelines,* Darlington, 2018.

Ellis, Samantha, *Take Courage: Anne Brontë and the Art of Life,* 2016.

Humphries, Patrick, *Bookends: The Simon and Garfunkel story.* Proteus Books, 1982.

Scott, P. J. M., *Anne Brontë:* A New Critical Assessment, 1983.

11

Blind Tom

'The Inexplicable Phenomenon'

The Blind Tom Egyptian Hall poster.

York Theatre Royal was the venue, in 1853, for a concert by Miss Elizabeth Taylor Greenfield, a black, former slave girl; reviews in the Yorkshire Gazette were very favourable.

In 1866 we heard that 'Blind Tom is Coming! Blind Tom, the Inexplicable Phenomenon', who had recently wowed audiences at the

St James's and Egyptian Halls in London (York Herald, 20 October). He too was an ex-slave and a protégé of Charles Dickens, who counted him as a 'valued friend'.

Born to enslaved parents in Columbus, Georgia, Thomas Wiggins was blind from birth and dismissed as a 'useless burden' by his enslavers. He reputedly was able to imitate sung melodies with astonishing accuracy by age two and to have been able to play the piano soon after, having learned by listening to the slave owner's daughters. He was also able to compose original tunes at a very early age. Tom was a 'make weight' thrown into the deal when his mother was bought by a tobacco-planter: 'a lump of black flesh born blind, and with the vacant grin of idiocy'. He turned out to be a success on the novelty and trick circuit: for example, 'his most confusing feat was to play one air with his left hand, another with his right in a different key, whilst he sang a third tune in a different key again... experts such as the Head of Music at Edinburgh testified to his accuracy.'

Despite his fame, one thing is certain: behind the headlines the story of Thomas Wiggins is a shameful, disturbing example of exploitation, racism, and abuse that is painful to hear and impossible to excuse or justify.

Canajoharie Wide-Awake Courier, 24 May 1892.

Tom is known to have influenced Dizzy Gillespie, Elton John, and T Bone Burnett.

https://klinkharthall.org/thomas-wiggins/

See:

Gustafson, Adam. 'The story of Elizabeth Taylor Greenfield, America's first black pop star'. The Conversation.

Chybowski, Julia J., 'Becoming the 'Black Swan' in mid-nineteenth-century America:: Elizabeth Taylor Greenfield's early life and debut concert tour'. Journal of the American Musicological Society. 67 (1): 125–165, 2014.

12

The Barber-Surgeons of York

For haircuts, teeth extraction and surgery

Barber-surgeons operating on a boil on a man's forehead (in the style of Miguel March).

Wellcome Collection ICV 17916 Full Bibliographic Record: http://catalogue.wellcomelibrary.org/record=b1202834.

It was the Barber-Surgeons of York (Ebor) who were responsible for professional medical training, professional standards and practitioner licensing in York until the establishment of the York Medical Society and York's first medical school. The first Barber (Rogerus le Barber) was admitted in 1290 – 18 years before the first recorded Barber of the London Company. The Exchequer accounts of York for 1346 tells us: 'Payments to William de Bolton and Hugo de Kilvington, Barber-Surgeons, going from York to the Castle of Bamburgh to heal the said David de Brus who lay there, having been wounded with an arrow at the said battle [Neville's Cross, 1346], and to extract the arrow and to heal him with despatch… £6.' David de Brus was the younger brother of Robert the Bruce, King of Scotland, and victor at Bannockburn. De Brus later became King David of Scotland. At any one time the Gild comprised 20 or so registered 'Barber-Surgeons' who cut hair, extracted teeth and performed all manner of surgical procedures. It took a seven-year apprenticeship in order to become a full member; apprentices were trained in the 'humours' in the body and the phases of the moon. The best time for blood-letting, for example, depended as much on the signs of the zodiac as anything physiological.

See:

Auden, G.A., 'The Gild of Barber Surgeons of the City of York', *Proceedings of the Royal Society of Medicine* 1928, 1400-1406.

Decamp, Eleanor, Sian, *Performing Barbers, Surgeons and Barber-Surgeons in Early Modern English Literature*, Pembroke College, University of Oxford, DPhil in English Literature Submission: Michaelmas 2011.

13

The York Observatory

Reaching for the stars

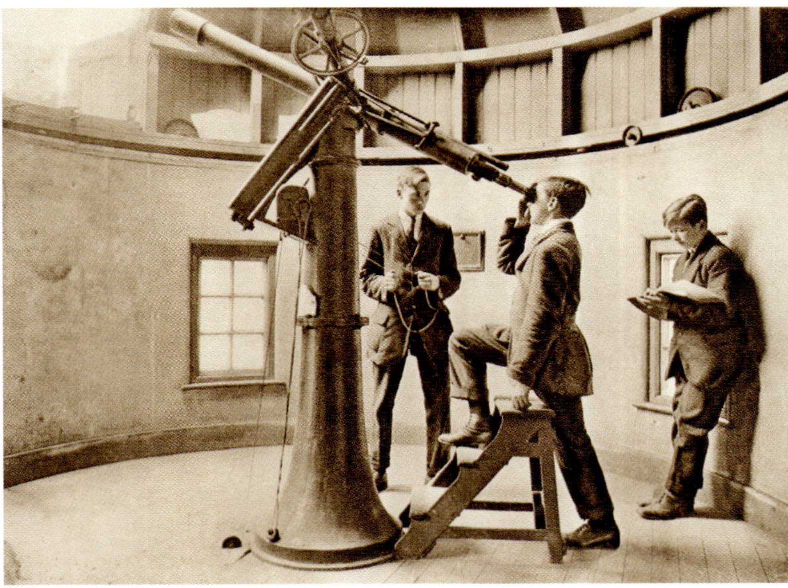

One of two 4ft refracting telescopes in Bootham School Observatory, York, in 1919, supplied by Cooke, Troughton & Simms. In 1850 Bootham was one of the UK's first schools to have its own observatory.

The Observatory in Museum Gardens was completed in 1833; its 4in refractor telescope was built by York's Thomas Cooke in 1850 before he went on to make what was then the largest telescope in the world. York played a crucial role in the development of astronomy in the 1780s when two prominent astronomers – the deaf and dumb John Goodricke (1764–86) and Edward Pigott laid the foundations of variable star astronomy – the study of stars of varying brightness. Goodricke has a college at the University of York named after him and Pigott was the first Englishman to discover a comet, which subsequently took his name. The Observatory also has an 1811 clock which tells the time based on the positions of stars. At one time it was the clock by which all others in York were set and is still always four minutes, 20 seconds behind GMT. In the mid-19th century you had to be a member of the Yorkshire Philosophical Society or it would cost you sixpence to check a timepiece against the Observatory Clock.

The York Observatory originated from a promise made at the very first meeting of the British Association for the Advancement of Science, which took place under the auspices of the Yorkshire Philosophical Society at the Yorkshire Museum in 1831. The Vice President of the Royal Astronomical Society, Dr Pearson, promised that if an observatory were built in York he would personally supply two of his best instruments. He duly obliged, also providing other scientific instruments – including the aforementioned clock. The conical roof was designed by John Smeaton, designer of the Eddystone Lighthouse. Today the observatory houses a telescope made by Thomas Cooke in 1850 with which you can see the stars and planets at night and safely observe the sun during the day.

Thomas Cooke: Telescope Man

Thomas Cooke came to York in 1829 and made his first telescope using the base of a whisky glass for a lens and a tin for the tube. In 1837 he opened his first instrument-making shop at 50 Stonegate with a loan of £100 from his wife's uncle. Cooke quickly gained a reputation for high quality and was soon making cutting-edge microscopes, opera glasses, spectacles, electrical machines, barometers, thermometers, globes, sundials and mathematical instruments as well as telescopes. By 1844 he had expanded and moved to 12 Coney Street. The firm later developed into Cooke, Troughton & Simms, based in Bishophill, and became part of Vickers Instruments, which was later sold to Bio-Rad, formerly in Haxby Road.

See:

Argyle, Robert W., 'Thomas Cooke (1807–1868)–A Great English Telescope Maker', *The Observatory,* 127: 392–400, 2007.

Lunn, Martin, 'Thomas Cooke: Telescope Maker of York,' pp.115–128 in Whitworth, 2000.

Whitworth, Alan,. *Aspects of York: Discovering Local History,* Barnsley, 2000.

14

Mutton Curry, Hangman

'Gin was apt to provide a snare for him.'

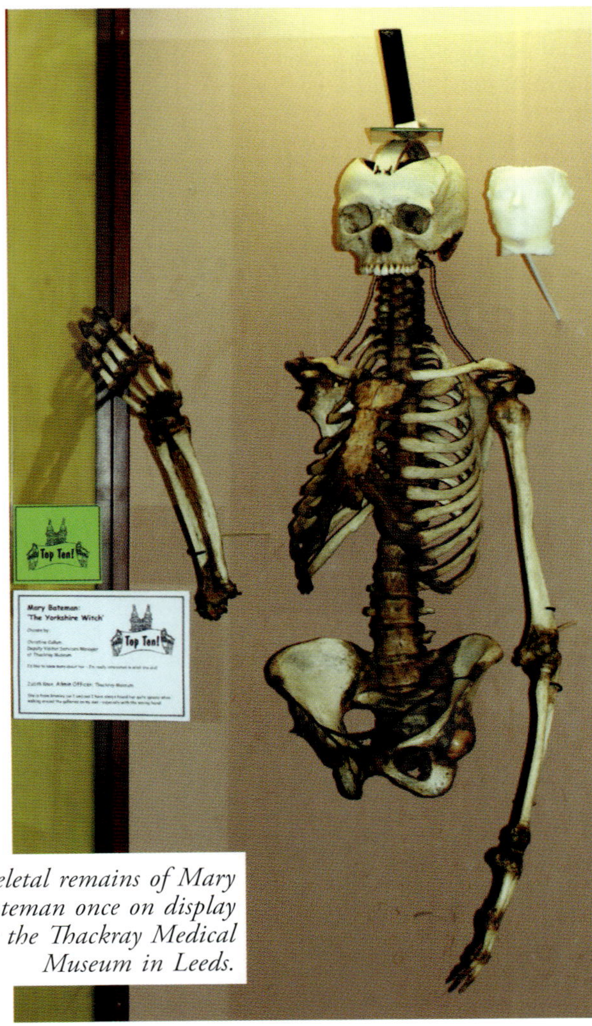

The skeletal remains of Mary Bateman once on display at the Thackray Medical Museum in Leeds.

William 'John' Curry (or Curry Wilkinson, or Thomas Askern) from Thirsk was the hangman for Yorkshire between 1802 and 1835 and carried out at least 58 and as many as 117 hangings during his 33-year reign of death. He was known as 'Mutton Curry' because he had twice been convicted of sheep stealing, having had his death sentence commuted on each occasion. The second time, in 1801, Curry was awaiting transportation. Fortunately, though, a hangman was urgently needed at York Castle and Curry was offered the job. By 1810 he had performed 25 executions, including a number of convicted Luddites from Cartwright's Mill at Rawfolds, as described in Charlotte Bronte's Shirley.

http://www.capitalpunishmentuk.org/early.html provides the detail and says it best:
A notable execution took place on the 20th of March 1809 when he hanged the 'Yorkshire Witch' Mary Bateman for the murder of Rebecca Perigo, alongside Joseph Brown who had killed Elizabeth Fletcher. The 16th of January 1813 was to be Curry's busiest day, with 14 men to hang. The executions were carried out in two groups, one at 11a.m. and one at 2p.m. in what was to be York's biggest ever hanging. A 'vast concourse' of people assembled on St George's Field to see this mass 'launch into eternity' as hangings were then known. The prisoners were Luddites who were trying to halt mechanisation of the textile industries of Yorkshire and Lancashire by violent means, as this was causing widespread unemployment and destitution. Following an attempt to destroy Cartwright's textile mill at Rawfold near Brighouse in April 1812, over 100 men had been rounded up. Sixty four were charged with a variety of offences and came before a special judicial commission at York Castle at the beginning of

January 1813. Twenty four of them were convicted and 17 sentenced to hang. The remainder were transported. The first of these executions was carried out on Friday the 8th of January when three men suffered for the murder of mill owner William Horsfall, including the Luddite's leader in Yorkshire, George Mellor, the remainder of the group being dealt with just over a week later.

On the 14th of April, 1821 Curry was called upon to perform two executions. First he hanged highwayman Michael Shaw at York Castle and then had to walk across town to execute William Brown for burglary at the City Gaol. He was somewhat drunk by the time he got there and while waiting on the platform for the prisoner to appear, he began shaking the noose at spectators, calling out to them: 'Some of you come up and I'll try it!

When Brown appeared, Curry had to be assisted by a warder and one of the sheriff's officers. 'The executioner, in a bungling manner and with great difficulty, being in a state of intoxication, placed the cap over the culprit's face and attempted several times to place the rope round his neck, but was unable.

'He missed the unfortunate man's head with the noose every time that he tried. The cap was each time removed from the malefactor's face, who stared wildly around upon the spectators,' The Times newspaper reported on the 24th of April. The crowd were not amused by this and called out 'Hang him, hang Jack Ketch'.

On the 1st of September 1821 Curry had to hang seven men at one time. The execution was reported by The Yorkshire Gazette as follows: 'On Saturday last, a few minutes before 12 o'clock, the unfortunate men were conducted from their cells to the fatal drop. After a short time spent in prayer they were launched into eternity. None of them seemed to suffer much.

'However, by an unaccountable neglect of the executioner (Curry) in not keeping sufficiently clear of the drop when the bolt was pulled out, he fell into the trap along with the malefactors.'

He retired, 20 hangings later, otium sine dignitate, to the Thirsk Poor House in 1835. The Yorkshire Gazette primly pointed out that 'gin was apt to provide a snare for him'.

See:

Peacock, A.J., William Curry – Hangman and Sheep-stealer, *York History 1*, 47-50.

www.capitalpunishmentuk.org/york.html

15

The Guild-book of the Barber-Surgeons of York

A rare survival of late mediaeval medical knowledge

Guild-book of the barber-surgeons of York, British Library.

This manuscript was made in the late 15th century for members of the Guild of Barber-Surgeons of the city of York and shows very clearly how mediaeval medical knowledge and practice was influenced by religion and astrology.

The British Library website (www.bl.uk/collection-items/guild-book--of-the-barber-surgeons-of-the-city-of-york) reveals:

Divided into two parts, one half of the manuscript features medical and astrological drawings and diagrams, including that of the Vein Man, the Zodiac Man (image no. 2), the Four Humours, and a circular zodiac chart, known as a volvelle (image no. 1), which has moving parts. The volvelle would have been used to predict the best time to provide medical treatment to a patient. The success of a particular remedy or operation was often considered dependent on assistance from religious saints: the volvelle is accompanied by illustrations of St John the Baptist, St John the Evangelist, and Sts Cosmas and Damian, the patron saints of doctors and surgery.

Publishers Boydell & Brewer add that it is:

A unique record of the knowledge, ambitions, activities and civic relationships maintained by the Barbers and Surgeons Guild over a period of 300 years. The manuscript's earliest folios contain images, astrological tracts, a plague treatise and a bloodletting poem. To these were added early modern ordinances and oaths, a series of royal portraits, and the names of the Guild's masters and apprentices. It is a rare survival of late medieval medical knowledge placed within a civic context.

See:

The Guild Book of the Barbers and Surgeons of York (British Library, Egerton MS 2572) Study and Edition
Edited by Richard D. Wragg, Boydell & Brewer

Margaret C Barnett, The Barber-Surgeons of York, *www.ncbi.nlm.nih.gov/pmc/articles/PMC1033769/pdf/medhist00144-0024.pdf*

16

Anne Lister

'Gentleman jack' in York

Watercolour portrait of Anne Lister of Shibden Hall. Probably the portrait painted by a Mrs Taylor on Wednesday, 20 to Thursday 21 November 1822, as described in Lister's diary:

Wednesday 20 November [Halifax] At 12:40, too George in the gig & drove to Mrs Taylor's. Sat for my likeness perhaps 1 1/4 hour. Very well satisfied with the sketch. There is something so very characteristic in the figure. Paid for it, 2 guineas... Neither Mrs Rawson nor Catherine thought it a good likeness. Found great fault with the mouth &, at first, with almost every part of the whole thing. Thursday 21 November [Halifax] ...Went to Mrs Taylor... sat nearly an hour during which she closed the mouth, improved the picture exceedingly & made it an admirable likeness... Got home at 2.25. The likeness struck me as so strong I could not help laughing. My aunt came up & laughed too, agreeing that the likeness was capital. Ditto my uncle. We are all satisfied, let others say what they may.

Anne Lister revealed her true feelings nine months later on 30 August 1823: 'Mrs Taylor's sketch of me, like a person afraid of speaking. Too foolish looking. Could not bear it. Not at all characteristic.'

Anne Lister (1791–1840) is commonly regarded as 'the first modern lesbian'. At the time, the word 'lesbian' was not a word to be found in the English lexicon. Lister's diaries, much of it written in code, 'detailed her romantic and sexual relationships with women, and were added to the UNESCO Memory of the World register in 2011, with the organisation recognising her 'comprehensive and painfully honest account of lesbian life.' The journals, amounting to more than four million words, were recognised as a 'pivotal' document in British history by the United Nations. They were not decrypted until long after her death, and the codebreaker was Helena Whitbread.

In July 2018 a rainbow plaque honouring Anne Lister was unveiled at Holy Trinity Church in Goodramgate. It commemorates Anne Lister's 'marital commitment' to Ann Walker on 30 March 1834 after Lister received the Church's blessing to privately contract a marriage to her. The blue plaque with rainbow edging is the city's first LGBT+ history plaque.

The Listers were a minor landowning family at Shibden in Calderdale, West Riding of Yorkshire. Anne had multiple lesbian affairs from when she was a schoolgirl, often on long trips abroad. In 1804, she was despatched to the Manor House School in York (then in what is now the King's Manor buildings), where Anne met her first love, Eliza Raine (1791–1860). Eliza was the illegitimate, half-Indian daughter of an East India Company surgeon from Madras, who was brought to Yorkshire after his death and set to inherit a substantial amount of money. Anne and Eliza shared an attic bedroom called 'The Slope' at the boarding school, which made the relationship with Eliza easy. Anne was asked to leave after two years.

Eliza had always expected to live with Anne when they left Manor School, but Anne began affairs with other women, including Isabella Norcliffe and Mariana Belcombe. A despairing and frustrated Eliza eventually was admitted to Clifton House Asylum in York, run by Mariana's father, William, in 1814, and was later transferred to Terrace House in Osbaldwick, where she died on 31 January 1860. She is buried in Osbaldwick churchyard just across the road.

Muscular and masculine to look at, dressed always in black, and highly educated, Anne Lister was later known, often pejoratively, as 'Gentleman Jack'. Her final relationship was with Ann Walker, to whom she was 'married' in Holy Trinity Church, Goodramgate, York, apparently now celebrated as 'the birthplace of lesbian marriage in Britain'. On gaining her inheritance (Shibden), Anne became a seasoned traveller. The website (https://www.annelister.co.uk/annes-travels/ tells how:

Mountaineering in the Pyrenees became a challenge to her, and in 1830 she was the first woman to ascend Mount Perdu, an achievement which was crowned by the even more difficult feat of completing, in 1838, the first ascent of Mount Vignemale and being not only the first woman, but also the first person, to do so.

Anne Lister died relatively young from an insect sting, at age 49, while travelling in Russia, at Koutais near Tiflis (now Tblisi) in Georgia. Her embalmed body was brought back to Shibden and she was buried in the Halifax parish church where she and her ancestors had worshipped for centuries.

Anne Lister College is one of the two new colleges on the University of York's Campus East. The accommodation and social hub buildings are surrounded by landscaped gardens and a large green space for university and college events.

'We're the first of the University of York's colleges to be named after a woman, as well as someone who was part of the LGBTQ+ community.

'We hope our students follow in Anne Lister's footsteps - by being broad in their knowledge and prolific in the pursuit of it, while being unashamedly themselves.'

Sunday, 24 January 2021, Changing city, Matt Ward-Perkins, as reported in https://yorkmix.com/revealed-the-groundbreaking-name-of-a-new-college-in-york/

See:

Whitbread, Helena, *I Know My Own Heart: The Diaries of Anne Lister 1791–1840,* Virago, 1988.

Whitbread, Helena, *No Priest But Love: Excerpts from the Diaries of Anne Lister,* NYU Press, 1993.

Choma, Anne, *Gentleman Jack: The Real Anne Lister,* Penguin Books & BBC Books, 2019.

Steidele, Angela, *Gentleman Jack. A Biography of Anne Lister: Regency Landowner, Seducer and Secret Diarist,* Serpent's Tail, London 2018. First published as Anne Lister. Eine erotische Biographie, Matthes & Seitz Berlin, 2017.

Vicinus, Martha, *Intimate Friends: Women Who Loved Women,* 1778–1928, Chicago, 2004.

17

Iucundus the Monk

Party animal

A monk sneaking a drink of wine. British Library Illumination from a copy of Li livres dou santé by Aldobrandino of Siena. British Library manuscript, Sloane 2435, f. 44v, late 13th century.

In the 15th century, before the Dissolution when a young monk called Iucundus joined the monks of St Leonard's Priory in York, little did he know it but he was making a life-changing mistake – the well-named novice (it means jolly) was rather bibulous and something of a party animal. He had made his intemperate decision 'in a fit of headache and remorse, after heavy potations on the occasion of the installation of a new Lord Mayor… The irrevocable vows were on him; for life he was bound to eat only vegetables and bread, drink very small beer, and sleep only six hours in the night.

'A year passed. The full paunch of Brother Iucundus began to subside; his fat cheeks to fall flabby, like the dewlaps of a cow; a dispirited expression took the place of the watery twinkle which had once animated his eye.'

Sarah Baring-Gould, Yorkshire Oddities, Incidents & Strange Events, fifth edition, 1900.

This life of asceticism did not sit well with him, so he compromised and decided to live a life of austerity all year long, apart from on one day:

Come what might, Brother Iucundus felt he must have a fling. He should die without it. Just one jollification in the twelvemonth, and then he would put up for the rest of the year with beans and cabbage, small beer and matins before dawn. York fair approached. York fair! of all that is ravishing! The shows of dancing dogs, the whirli-go-rounds, the giantesses and dwarfs, the 'spice' stalls, the drinking-booths! To York fair he must, he would go, if condemned to a bean and a thimbleful of water for fasting dinner ever after.

This day happened to coincide with York Fair – never a sober event – to which Iucundus duly headed and truly let down what was left of his hair. He stole the Priory keys from the porter's lodge, pocketed a crown from the Prior's room and set off for his day of unalloyed joy.

Iucundus had enjoyed himself amazingly. The amount of gingerbread horses and men he had consumed was prodigious. He had seen 'The Spotted Boy' and 'The Bearded Woman'; he had gone round in the whirligig on the back of a wooden horse; he had shot for nuts at a mark, and won his pocket full, which he cracked every now and then, and washed down with a draft of really good ale. And now, just now, he was going up in the boat of a great see-saw, with a foaming tankard in his hand, his jolly red face illumined with glee …

The following day he was wheeled home in a barrow and tried for his permissiveness – his punishment was to be walled alive into a niche in the Priory cellar.

Immuration was fairly low down on Iucundus's list of things to do before he met his maker; his struggle to save himself resulted in the wall collapsing, through which he tumbled into St Mary's Abbey immediately next door. Before long he became a Benedictine monk there and a paragon of sobriety.

One year or so later, Iucundus was appointed keeper of the cellar; unfortunately, or fortunately perhaps, this cellar was a wine cellar and, soon after his appointment, Iucundus was found comatose at the wrong end of a barrel of claret: his punishment was, again, to be immured at the scene of the crime, which happened to be the exact place through which he had tumbled from the Priory next door. His former colleagues heard the commotion he made, tore down the walls and were confronted by the miracle that was Iucundus. So stupefied where they that they made him Prior of St Leonard's.

A monk sneaking a drink of wine. British Library Illumination from a copy of Li livres dou santé by Aldobrandino of Siena. British Library manuscript, Sloane 2435, f. 44v, late 13th century.

See:

https://en.wikisource.org/wiki/Yorkshire_Oddities,_Incidents_and_Strange_Events/Brother_Jucundus

Chrystal, Paul, *York's Churches and Places of Worship*, Catrine, 2016.

18

York Medical Society

'Promoting and diffusing medical knowledge'

York Medical Society – the old library

York Medical Society was founded at 23 Stonegate by seven medical men in 1832 for 'the purpose of promoting and diffusing medical knowledge'. This was intended to build on the work of the York Gild of Barber-Surgeons, who had looked after the training and licensing of medical practitioners, standards of treatment and professional education in the city from the 14th century. The minutes of the society provide a fascinating record of rapid changes in medicine, diagnosis, epidemiology and social change, all reflected in the lectures given there over the years. The society was active in driving social change and in improving living conditions: a paper from 1842 entitled A Plan of Political Medicine anticipated the ethos and practicalities of the National Health Service by over 100 years. York's pre-eminence in psychiatric medicine and patient care (as exemplified by the Retreat) is reflected in the society's work.

There were also close links with York's first Medical School, which thrived between 1834 and 1858. Indeed, the annual Oration and other lectures were the main source of postgraduate medical education in the city for many years. Much of the timber-framed house goes back to 1590 (as evidenced by the dated lead rain-water head over the entrance doors – the oldest surviving in York), although parts such as the wing known as Little Paradise to the left of the entrance and one of the fireplaces are older still. Extensive alterations and additions took place in the 17th and 18th centuries. A dispensary and consulting rooms were developed and the west wing was added by Dr Tempest Anderson; the speaking tube from Dr Anderson's bed to the front door to address night callers can still be seen. Sales of the properties bought by Anderson's family after his death paid for the wing he bequeathed to the Yorkshire Philosophical Society at the Yorkshire Museum. The Yorkshire Law Society, established in 1786 and the second oldest Law Society in the UK, set up its library here in 1944.

The website tells us:

York Medical Society Collection is made up of nearly 2,000 titles including books from the York dispensatory (303 items) and York County Hospital medical library. There are also over 30 journal titles in the collection.

Treasures include:

- *William Hunter's* Anatomia uteri humani gravida tabulis illustrate *(1774)*
- *An almost complete run of the British Medical Journal from 1855 to 1950*
- *First edition of the collected works of Gabriello Fallopio, after whom the Fallopian Tube is named, published in Frankfurt in 1584*

- *2 v. ed. Works of Hippocrates in Latin published in Basle in 1564 with clasped binding and annotations in Greek filling the margins*
- *Thomas Addison's* On the constitutional and local effects of disease of the supra-renal capsules, *London 1855*

The books were deposited at the University of York in 2004 where they are held on deposit for the York Medical Society. Most of the material in the collection is catalogued and can be accessed via the University of York's online catalogue.

Milnes-Walker Collection

The website informs us:

> *The Milnes Walker collection consists of 200 early medical books, most of which were related to Wakefield and which cover a period of almost 450 years.*
>
> *The earliest book in the catalogue is 1538 and the latest, 1970. A few items date from the 16th century being mainly commentaries on Hippocrates, Galen and Dioscorides; the greatest number are by 17th and 18th century writers such as:*
>
> - *Thomas Sydenham, one of the most innovative physicians of the 17th century*
> - *John Huxham, notable for his studies of fevers*
> - *Richard Morton who studied tuberculosis*
> - *John Floyer, best known for introducing the practice of pulse rate measurement*
> - *Richard Mead, who helped towards a better understanding of transmissible diseases.*

The books were the gift of Robert Milnes Walker (b. 1903), Professor Emeritus of Surgery in the University of Bristol. He inherited them from his father, John William Walker (b.1859), who had bought the books at a sale at the beginning of the 20th century. John William Walker was the son of Thomas Walker, who was a Wakefield surgeon. Bookplates represent Wakefield medical circulating library and the Wakefield medical library which belonged to the Clayton Hospital, and was probably housed in the Wakefield dispensatory. Wakefield general dispensatory was established in 1787 and the library was probably originally housed there. A catalogue for the Wakefield medical library exists in the West Yorkshire Record Office.

The Retreat Collection

Borthwick also:

...have the archive of the Retreat, the independent psychiatric hospital opened by the Society of Friends in 1796, which became world famous for its mild methods of treating the insane - much of this archive has now been digitised and is available to view online.

York Minster Library, XVI. O. 10 was written in the fifteenth century and contains a collection of medical and culinary recipes. The forty-three folios that comprise this manuscript were described and examined in a work entitled 'A Medieval Book of Herbs and Medicine' written by Elizabeth Brunskill, a former library assistant, and from which a copy is held in York Minster Library's Special Collections.

York Minster Library, XVI. E. 32, or the York medical manuscript is a fifteenth-century compilation composed of a series of therapeutic texts intended to cure diseases or conditions. The majority of these texts are collections of herbal recipes which offer a number of treatments to cure various maladies. It also contains other practical texts which a medical practitioner would have found very useful to treat, diagnose and prognosticate diseases and their outcomes, including bloodletting instructions, herbals or a urine treatise.

See:

https://www.york.ac.uk/library/collections/named-collections/yorkmedicalsociety/

York Medical Society Catalogue, 1961.

Rules and Catalogue of Books of the Wakefield Medical Library, December 1872. (Printed in Wakefield by BW Allen, Market Place 1872; housed in the West Yorkshire Record Office.)

'Medicine in seventeenth-century *Yorkshire', Yorkshire Archaeology Journal,* 1946, 36, pp. 288-296.

A Fifteenth-Century Medical Handbook in York Minster Library (YML, XVI. E. 32). Part 1 – a blog by Dr Rebeca Cubas-Peña.

19

The Millennium Bridge

Cycle wheels for cyclists

The bridge is at the southern end of the New Walk.

York's newest bridge (opened in 2001) spanning the River Ouse is the elegant Millennium Bridge, inspired by the spokes of a bicycle and costing £2.4 million. The towerless 150m-length bridge, with its 80m inclined arm main span, is for the use of pedestrians and cyclists only. The bridge was soon attracting over 2,000 users per day, with half of these being cyclists. Here it is during the Christmas floods in 2015; the photographer is Dr Rachael Chrystal.

20

The Bolton Book of Hours

A book of Hours, attributed to 'Studio of unknown French (illuminator)', possibly in the style of an unknown Flemish (illuminator), c.1470 (creation date). Book of Hours (Horae Beatae Mariae Virginis in Usum Ecclesiae Romanae cum Calendario), Folio 86v: Hours of the Virgin: Compline: Entombment, overall, left, with Folio 87r at right. Illumination, Leaf (component), Manuscript. Place: Trinity College, Watkinson Library (Hartford, Connecticut, USA).

The stunning Bolton/Blackburn Hours was made for a citizen of York in around 1415 (York Minster Library Add. Ms. 2). It contains 47 full-page images depicting standing saints with their attributes, which, as Kathleen Scott points out, is the greatest number of miniatures in any surviving English book of hours.

Kathryn Margaret Rudy explains:

They are distributed sporadically throughout the manuscript, with little obvious relationship to the texts they face. The manuscript also contains 5 smaller miniatures, 16 historiated initials, and 11 full borders. Recent studies have productively contextualized its patronage, its didactic function, its 'hypertext', its relationship with local politics in York, with pilgrimage, and the meaning of a confessional prayer inscribed on its beginning and end leaves.

In their *Reconciliation and Family Values*, Professors Sarah Rees Jones and Felicity Riddy remind us that the 'rare and richly illuminated manuscript' Bolton Book was published at a fraught time in York's history which saw the execution of its archbishop, Richard Scrope:

One of the most commonly owned prayer books among the well-to-do laity in the Middle Ages, a Book of Hours set out the prayers for each liturgical hour of the day – hence the name. Calendars, prayers, psalms and masses for certain holy days were often included as well as the names of saints and prominent deceased family members.

Jones and Riddy provide the historical and religious context:

The most intriguing aspect of the book is its reference to Richard Scrope, Archbishop of York. In 1405 he led a northern rebellion against King Henry IV, was arrested at Pontefract, tried at Bishopthorpe Palace and beheaded. This was the first time that a lay court had ordered the execution of a prelate. In the aftermath, families in the city were torn apart in their support for one side or the other and there was an urgent need for a reconciliation to prevent further unrest.

Jones and Riddy argue that the Bolton Book of Hours was used as a vehicle for imagining and promoting harmony, both private and public, locally and nationally. Within a few years of his death, Richard Scrope came to be venerated as a cult figure with a saintly status.

See:

Jones, Sarah Rees, *Reconciliation and family values: How the Bolton Book of Hours helped to calm the storm of rebellion in medieval York* (www.york.ac.uk/news-and-events/features/bolton/)

Rudy, Kathryn Margaret. *The Bolton/Blackburn Hours (York Minster Add. Ms. 2): A New Solution to its Text-Image Disjunctions using a Structural Model.*

Luxford, Julian (ed), *Studies in Gothic Art, Architecture and Ideas,* Turnhout: Brepols, Harvey Miller, 2021.

Wieck, Roger *S. Painted Prayers: The Book of Hours in Medieval and Renaissance Art,* New York: George Braziller, 2004.

Calkins, Robert G. *Illuminated Books of the Middle Ages.* Ithaca, New York: Cornell University Press, 1983.

21

Alcuin and the Lost Library

Aristotle, Cicero and Virgil and Pliny –
the Vikings destroyed them all.

Raban Maur (left), supported by Alcuin (middle), dedicates his work to Archbishop Otgar of Mainz (Right). Manuscript: Wien, Österreichische Nationalbibliothek, cod.652, fol. 2v (Fulda, second quarter of the 9th century).

Alcuin (735CE-804CE), born in York, spent most of his celebrated life in York and was master of the Minster School. He went on to teach at Charlemagne's palace in Aachen and is one of the founding fathers of European culture. He describes York in his *On the Saints of the Church of York: '... My heart is set to praise my home And briefly tell the ancient cradling Of York's famed city through the charms of verse.'* Alcuin's extensive library was one of the best and biggest in the world and helped York to become one of the premier seats of learning in the eight century.

The Old Palace not only houses York Minster's library and archives but also the collections department and the conservation studio. It is known as the Old Palace because part of the building used to be the chapel of the 13th-century Archbishop's palace. In 1810 it was refurbished and, shortly after, the Minster's collection was installed there. The original library was the dream and ambition of King Egbert, a disciple of the Venerable Bede: he opened a school of international repute and started a collection of books. The librarianship then passed, from 778–781, to Flaccus Albinus Alcuinus, Alcuin. He later became one of the architects of the Carolingian Renaissance. Alcuin's catalogue featured works by many of the Church Fathers and classical authors such as Pliny, Aristotle, Cicero and Virgil – but all was tragically lost when the Minster and library were sacked by the Vikings. It was not until the 18th century that the collection started to grow significantly: from 1716 to 1820, there were more than 1,200 loans by 179 different borrowers. Laurence Sterne, author of *The Life and Opinions of Tristram Shandy, Gentleman,* was a regular user. By 1810 there were nearly 8,000 volumes and the library moved to its present home in Dean's Park; in 1890 Edward Hailstone bequeathed 10,000 volumes.

Historian John Boswell cited Alcuin's writings as demonstrating a personal outpouring of his internalised homosexual feelings. Others agree that Alcuin at times 'comes perilously close to communicating openly his same-sex desires,' (Coon, 2011) and this reflects the erotic subculture of the Carolingian monastic school, but also perhaps a 'queer space' where 'erotic attachment and affections may be safely articulated'. According to David Clark, passages in some of Alcuin's writings can be seen to display homosocial desire, even possibly homoerotic imagery. However, he argues that it is not possible to necessarily determine whether they were the result of an outward expression of erotic feelings on the part of Alcuin (Clark 2009).

See:

Boswell, John, *Christianity, Social Tolerance, and Homosexuality: Gay People in Western Europe from the Beginning of the Christian Era to the Fourteenth Century,* Chicago, 2015.

Clark, David, *Between Medieval Men: Male Friendship and Desire in Early Medieval English Literature,* Oxford, 2009.

Coon, Lynda L., *Dark Age Bodies: Gender and Monastic Practice in the Early Medieval West.* University of Pennsylvania Press, 2011.

Alcuin College at the University of York is named after him.

22

York Minster Library

The archives and manuscripts occupy a kilometre of shelving

From the York Gospels. Open at folios 85v–86r, beginning the book of Luke: on the left, St. Luke is pictured writing his gospel, blessed by the hand of God from above. On the right, the gospel opens with a splendidly decorated gold capital Q(uoniam) with a dragon as its tail, gold display letters completing the incipit.

York Minster holds the largest cathedral library in England in the Archbishop's Palace Chapel with over 125,000 volumes and is recognised as the most important cathedral library in Britain. The York Minster website (https://yorkminster.org/discover/collections-archive-library/) reveals that the collections of archives and manuscripts date back to the year 1000, and occupy a kilometre of shelving:

> *We hold the archives of the Chapter of York, including the fabric rolls, which document the construction of the Minster. We also hold prints, plans and drawings of the building and surrounding land. Our manuscript collections span the last millennium, with examples on display in the Undercroft including the 1,000-year-old York Gospels.*

The palace, built between 1154 and 1181, was the main residence of the archbishops of York until Walter de Gray bought Bishopthorpe in 1241 and moved out there. Archbishops ever since have followed him.

York is one of the earliest surviving examples of a building specifically designed to house a library, built 600 years ago, when it was becoming *de riguer* for cathedrals to have their own libraries.

York's is the largest cathedral library in the country, closely linked with the University of York since 1964 and now with more than 125,000 books, on topics ranging from local history; early York printing; Civil War tracts (2,000 items mainly relating to Yorkshire); theology through the ages; church history and architecture. The largest archive collection is that of the Dean and Chapter's own archive, dating from c.1150 to the present, and those of the College of the Vicars Choral, c.1200–1936; the Song School; and the archaeological archive of excavations of the Minster from 1967 onwards.

Over 25,000 of the volumes are pre-1800, and the library also holds 115 incunables (works printed before 1501). The library also holds special collections including a comprehensive collection of material on the history of York and Yorkshire; stained glass; a collection of 16th–20th-century printed and manuscript music; and a large collection of 18th and 19th-century theatre playbills, and newspapers. The Yorkshire collections, totalling some 20,000 books and pamphlets, is the most comprehensive collection of earlier material for Yorkshire, with York and Yorkshire printing. Modern books include theology, church history and the history of the Minster and city. An extension was added to accommodate the increasing number of volumes in 1997.

Non-manuscript material includes: maps and plans of Yorkshire; architectural plans of the Minster and its properties; and photographs, mainly of the Minster and York. Music collections include: manuscript and printed music, with some mediaeval liturgical music, mainly relating to York. The unique printed copy of Byrd's *Gradualia* (1605), and manuscript and printed music by Purcell; the Minster choir repertoire from c.1600 to the present day and compositions by Minster organists.

Most famous is the beautifully illustrated *York Gospels,* brought to the Minster in 1020; it is used as the oath book for all incoming Archbishops and Minster clergy and is on display in the undercroft of the Minster. In addition to the four gospels, it contains the oaths taken by the deans and canons, documents about land ownership and the letter of King Cnut (r.1016–1035). The book was produced at Canterbury c. 1000 and came to York with Archbishop Wulfstan around 1020.

John Neuton, born c. 1350, treasurer of York Minster from 1385 until his death in 1414, was the driving force behind today's magnificent collection. He bequeathed a collection of books which went some way to replacing those destroyed by the Vikings.

In 1421–22 Neuton's books were labelled and fixed to the reading desks with chains.

See:

Stephen, Lewis *(The treasures of York Minster Library,* York Press, 29 November 2008.

Chrystal, Paul, *The Book – How the knowledge of the past was preserved,* Barnsley, 2023.

23

Samuel Tuke, Rev Sydney Smith and the Retreat

'An institution for the care and proper treatment of those labouring under… the loss of reason'

Restraining equipment at the time of York Lunatic Asylum scandal; Science Museum

The Rev D Sydney Smith's (1771–1845) entry in the *Dictionary of National Biography* describes him as 'author and wit'. His relevance to York comes in his lengthy and detailed review in the *Edinburgh Review* of Samuel Tuke's (1784–1857) *'Description of the Retreat,'* published in 1813, which his father, Henry, had urged him to publish, based on his experiences of the Retreat. Smith highly praised the Retreat and Samuel Tuke's book, giving both much-needed, impartial publicity, in the face of the 'vehement detraction' both attracted, because 'The work directed attention to the abuses common in the madhouses of the period, and exerted a strong influence in the direction of urgently required reform.' Indeed, the head of York County Asylum in Bootham, in defence of the 'old system' and his inhumane institution, wrote anonymously to a local newspaper 'which raised a controversy that only died when that asylum was purged of abominable abuses at the instance of Godfrey Higgins actively supported by the Tuke family.'

William Tuke founded the Retreat in 1796: in doing so he instigated a revolutionary way of treating people with mental health conditions: humanely. This was in stark contrast to existing methods, which saw patients as being in possession of demons, chained up as criminals – prisoners rather than patients in a squalid, punitive environment. Tuke wanted 'an institution for the care and proper treatment of those labouring under that most afflictive dispensation, the loss of reason'. His resolve was galvanised when Friends (Quakers) who had been asked to visit a widow Quaker patient, Hannah Mills. She had been transferred from Leeds to York Lunatic Asylum, but the Friends in York were refused visiting rights. Hannah died there on 30 April 1790. William's daughter, Ann Tuke, heard of this and demanded answers from her father as to why Quakers could not have their own asylum. The 30-bed Retreat or, to give it its full name, the Retreat for Persons Afflicted with Disorders of the Mind, as suggested by Mary Maria Tuke, was the result. It was financed largely by donations from local Quakers. The Retreat on Lamel Hill, which, until 2018, served the needs of psychiatric patients as a highly respected centre of excellence in mental health medicine. However, on 31 December 2018, it withdrew from inpatient care with its remaining services for eating disorders and personality disorders now being run by the Schoen Clinic. The Retreat continues to run outpatient community psychological assessment, diagnostic and therapy services at the Tuke Centre, including an Autism and ADHD service.

According to York Civic Trust,

From 1806–28 Smith was rector of Foston-le-Clay, an isolated parish 'twelve miles from a lemon,' near Castle Howard. In 1808, he reluctantly moved his family to Yorkshire. Because there had been no resident rector at Foston for 150 years, and no habitable rectory, he lived in Heslington from 1809–14, [in More House] what, with a benign irony that he would have relished, is now the Roman Catholic Chaplaincy of the University of York.

A blue plaque celebrates Smith's residence there. Sydney Smith Court is in Heslington.

In the review, Smith wrote: 'his book does him [Tuke] very great credit; it is full of good sense and humanity, right feelings and rational views… the great principle on which it [the Retreat] appears to be conducted, is that of kindness to the patients.'

York Lunatic Asylum, described as *'a state of filth horrible beyond description'* was designed by the celebrated John Carr, but that's where the good news stops. It opened in 1777 on Bootham with 15 patients, rising to 199 by 1813. Its mission was to be caring 'without undue severity'. The Asylum advertised that, *'patients are admitted according to their circumstances, the terms for pauper patients belonging to the City, Ainsty and County are 8 shillings per week'.*

Part of the asylum burnt down in 1814, with the tragic loss of four patients, and all patient records; somewhat convenient, perhaps, as the fire coincided with allegations of mis-management and the rise of the Retreat. All Bootham staff were dismissed and replaced. In the same year a visiting magistrate reported that the *'house is yet in a shocking state… a number of secret cells in a state of filth horrible beyond description,'* and the floor covered 'with straw perfectly soaked with urine and excrement'. In 1904 it was renamed Bootham Park Hospital. It is now closed and currently empty.

See:

Evert A Duyckinck, *The Wit and Wisdom of the Rev. Sydney Smith,* 2022.

Paul Chrystal, *The Rowntree Family of York,* 2013.

Paul Chrystal, *Rowntrees: The Early History,* 2021.

Hesketh Pearson, *The Smith of Smiths, Being the Life, Wit and Humour of Sydney Smith,* London, 2009.

https://kyhi.org/2021/06/15/the-historical-use-of-restraints-in-asylums/

WH Auden (ed.), *The Selected Writings of Sydney Smith,* New York, 1956.

Peter Virgin, *Sydney Smith,* London, 1994.

Digby, Anne (1985). *Madness, Morality and Medicine: A Study of the York Retreat 1796–1914.* Cambridge

Tuke, Samuel [1813] (1996). *Description of the Retreat. London: Process Press*

24

Dr John Sentamu

'Once upon a time you couldn't really be living in poverty if you had a regular income, you could find yourself on a low income, yes. But that is no longer so. You can be in work and still live in poverty'

Dr Sentamu with his tent in St John's Chapel, York Minster, during a seven-day fast and prayer vigil for peace in the Middle East in 2006. (Church Times)

John Tucker Mugabi Sentamu, Baron Sentamu, was born on 10 June 1949 and is a retired Anglican bishop and life peer. He was Archbishop of York and Primate of England from 2005 to 2020.

Born near in Masooli village, Kampala, in Uganda, the sixth of 13 children, Sentamu studied law at Makerere University before becoming an advocate of the Supreme Court of Uganda. Speaking out against the regime of President Idi Amin, he was detained for 90 days, and in 2007 he described how during that time he had been 'kicked around like a football and beaten terribly,' saying 'the temptation to give up hope of release was always present'. He fled as an immigrant to the United Kingdom in 1974, beginning his study of theology at Selwyn College, Cambridge, in 1976 and eventually gaining a doctorate in 1984. He studied for ordination at Ridley Hall, Cambridge, and was ordained in 1979. In 1996 he was area bishop of Stepney and in 2002 became Bishop of Birmingham. It was around this time that he served as advisor to the Stephen Lawrence Judicial Enquiry, and in 2002 he chaired the Damilola Taylor review. In 2005 John Sentamu was appointed Archbishop of York, enthroned at York Minster on 30 November 2005 (the feast of Saint Andrew), at a colourful and rhythmic ceremony with African singing and dancing, and contemporary music, with Sentamu himself playing African drums during the service. For a week in August 2006 (see image) Sentamu camped in York Minster, forgoing food in solidarity with those affected by the Middle East conflict, especially the children and other civilians killed and injured during the 2006 Lebanon War, when cluster bombs were used by Israeli forces.

In October 2018, Sentamu announced his retirement, scheduled for 7 June 2020. In June 2019, he ordained his wife as a deacon. Sentamu moved with his wife to Berwick and, on 14 June 2021, was licensed an honorary assistant bishop of the Diocese of Newcastle.

Some John Sentamu sentiments:

Poverty

For the very first time the majority of households in poverty in Britain have at least one person working. The nature of poverty in Britain is changing dramatically. For millions of hard-pressed people, work is no longer a route out of poverty. [...] Low pay is a scourge on our society, and we all pay for it. Low pay costs the taxpayer between 3.6 and 6 billion pounds a year in tax credits, in-work benefits and lost tax receipts. And as disposable income available to the lowest paid reduces, so too does the demand in the economy.

Malnutrition

Sentamu believes that food poverty is causing malnutrition in the UK. In 2013, he said that 'last year more than 27,000 people were diagnosed as suffering from malnutrition in Leeds – not Lesotho, not Liberia, not Lusaka but Leeds,' and feels these reports 'disgrace us all, leaving a dark stain on our consciences'.

Stop and search

In 2000, Sentamu, then Bishop of Stepney, was stopped by a City of London Police officer near St Paul's Cathedral. Sentamu claimed it was the eighth time he had been questioned by police in eight years, and that he was the only Church of England bishop to have been stopped by police in this way. In a 2010 debate in the House of Lords, Sentamu was critical of the standards of 'reasonable grounds to suspect' applied by police.

Robert Mugabe

On 9 December 2007, during a live television interview with Andrew Marr on BBC One, Sentamu made a very visible protest against Zimbabwean president Robert Mugabe. Sentamu took the white insert off his clerical shirt and cut it up, stating that:

> *As an Anglican, this is what I wear to identify myself that I'm a clergyman. Do you know what Mugabe has done? He's taken people's identity and literally, if you don't mind, cut it to pieces. This is what he's actually done, to a lot of – and in the end there's nothing. So as far as I'm concerned from now on, I'm not going to wear a dog collar until Mugabe's gone.*

See:

Encyclopaedia of World Biography 'John Sentamu biography', 2021.

Heraldic shields of Scrope and associated families, St Andrews church, Castle Combe

25

Archbishop Richard Scrope

Arrested and executed as a traitor

In 1399 Richard II, a friend of the city of York who had ruled for more than 20 years, was overthrown by Henry Bolingbroke of the House of Lancaster(later Henry IV).

The Archbishop of York, Richard Scrope, was executed in 1405 by Henry IV for his rebellion after the victory over Richard II. Henry rallied a group of supporters, overthrew and imprisoned Richard II, and usurped the throne. Henry had to contend with a number of rebellions, not least in the north of England, where the powerful Earl of Northumberland, Henry Percy, and his son 'Harry Hotspur' Percy sowed dissent.

, Richard Scrope was at the centre of all of this. He openly supported the traitors' cause and preached against the king in the Minster. The people responded and 'almost all the citizens of York capable of bearing arms' joined the rebels. At the end of May 1405, Archbishop Scrope was at the head of an army of 8,000 men, facing a large loyalist army on Shipton Moor. Henry marched on York, determined to 'wipe it off the face of the earth'. Scrope disbanded his force in exchange for a truce but was immediately arrested and executed as a traitor.

Miracles were seen in the Minster, which led to a shaken Henry banning all services for a year. His death from leprosy in 1413 was seen as divine retribution for the murder of an archbishop.

See:

McNiven, Peter, 'Scrope, Richard (c.1350–1405)', *Oxford Dictionary of National Biography* (online ed.), Oxford University Press, 2004.

Bevan, Bryan, *Henry IV*, New York: St. Martin's Press, 1994.

26

Rosalind Howard and her Teetotal Castle

'A fearless champion of causes' (The Times)

Castle Howard today.

Cecilia and her husband, George Howard, first opened Castle Howard, 15 miles north of York, to the public in 1952. It remains a private residence and has been the home of the Carlisle branch of the Howard family for more than 300 years. Castle Howard is not a castle as such: 'castle' is sometimes used, as here, to describe an English country house that was built on the site of a former castle. The building of Castle Howard began in 1699, with design work by playwright John Vanbrugh and Nicholas Hawksmoor. The estate had its own railway station from 1845 to the 1950s.

Rosalind Frances Howard, Countess of Carlisle (née Stanley, 1845–1921), known as the Radical Countess, was a promoter of women's political rights and an active ambassador for the temperance movement. On 4 October 1864 she married the painter George Howard, who became a Liberal MP from 1879. Personal and political disagreements drove the Howards apart, with Rosalind preferring to stay at their country houses, Castle Howard and her favourite home Naworth Castle near Brampton in Cumbria. She joined the Liberal Party women's associations and the temperance movement, involved herself in the management of the extensive family estates and took part in local government. She took the temperance pledge in 1881 and started demanding teetotalism from her tenants and closing down public houses on her estates the next year.

In 1890 Lady Carlisle became a member of the Women's Liberal Federation and persuaded the organisation to support extending the suffrage to all women, but denounced Pankhurst suffragettes' violent methods. She presided over the federation from 1894 until 1902 and again from 1906 until 1915. She was elected president of the British Women's Temperance Association in 1903 (later the White Ribbon Association) and president of the World's Woman's Christian Temperance Association in 1906.

Given her commitment to temperance, Rosalind, in the words of Daisy Dunn, 'set about her mission to dry the country out'. She lobbied unsuccessfully against legislation promoting the licensing of alcohol and bought pubs in Brampton near Naworth, converting them into temperance cafes. Most spectacularly, Rosalind decided it would be quite wrong to have any alcohol on the premises at Castle Howard, so she had the wine cellars cleared of all bottles. The tops were knocked off and the contents poured into one of the lakes. Anyone who has seen the television adaptation of Waugh's *Brideshead Revisited* may remember the scene in which Charles Ryder and Sebastian find the cellars devoid of wine – apart from one alcove containing a number of vintages in need of drinking. Back in the real world, the press, in an expression of fake news, got hold of the temperance story and reported that 1,000 bottles had been drained into a hole when they could have gone to soldiers in hospitals.

Any anxiety over Rosalind's social conscience can be dispelled when we remember that she made provision for 12 poverty-stricken women each month, who were granted free accommodation on the estate, and she organised holidays there for local children, including those from workhouses. She also supported miners as well as female suffrage, and championed the election of women to positions of influence in educational bodies.

Though she worked hard to improve the working-class people's living conditions, she was an elitist who resented the proletariats' involvement in democracy.

See:

Dunn, Daisy, *Not Far from Brideshead: Oxford between the Wars,* London, 2022.

Sex and Suffrage: The Life and Times of Rosalind Howard, Castle Howard, 12 July 2012.

Henley, Dorothy, *Rosalind Howard, Countess of Carlisle,* Hogarth Press, 1958.

Roberts, Charles, *The Radical Countess,* Steel Bros, 1962.

27

The Magnificent York Art Gallery Ceiling

There's just as much up there as there is down here

The magnificent ceiling and Clare Twomey's piece, Manifest: 10,000 hours, has been installed in the middle of the Centre of Ceramic Art's hall.

Until the re-opening of the York Gallery after its magnificent £8m refurbishment in 2013, very few people were aware of the hidden treasure concealed behind a false ceiling, accessed only by a little door off the Victorian building's narrow first-floor gallery. The treasure? A magnificent ceiling lost to public gaze since the 1940s and now exposed in all its glory. The website explains: 'A new mezzanine floor is set back from the front of the building, allowing visitors to enjoy the impact of the hall's original and full 15m height as well as its decorative trusses and ornate plaster work.'

Daylight flooding in from the overhead skylights above is enhanced by a wall of fan light windows. This makes the mezzanine gallery too bright for paintings, but it is the perfect space for the museum's extensive collection of British ceramics – at over 6,000 pieces the largest in the world, spanning pre-history to the present day. Clare Twomey's piece, *Manifest: 10,000 hours,* has been installed in the middle of the Centre of Ceramic Art's (CoCA's) hall. The artist created 10,000 ceramic bowls for the piece, commissioned especially for the gallery's opening. Two original marble columns were uncovered and restored in the entranceway; outside landscaped public gardens give visitors time and space for reflection. The side exterior has been clad in 300 hexagonal ceramic tiles in varying shades of blue.

In the gallery, every year between 1950 and 1962 an artist was paid £50 to produce a picture of York: L.S. Lowry's painting of Clifford's Tower is one of the results.

Laurence Stephen Lowry, R.A. (1887-1976) Clifford's Tower, York pencil on paper sketch for the famous painting.

See:

Riddick, Sarah, *York Through the Eyes of the Artist,* York, 1990.

28

Sheriff Hutton Castles

'few villages touch our national history so closely as Sheriff Hutton' (John Rushton, The Ryedale Story)

Sheriff Hutton castle today, taken from the east side of the castle (artist unknown).

Ten miles north of York, on the way to Castle Howard, Sheriff Hutton has always enjoyed royal connections and has always had at least one castle. Bertram de Bulmer built the first castle in the village during the reign of King Stephen (1135–54). After the civil war between Stephen and Matilda (1138–53), the castle and manor were seized by the Crown before being held for the king by the Mauley family. The manor eventually came into the possession of the Neville family in the 14th century, until 1480, when it was surrendered to the crown.

During the reign of King Stephen, a motte-and-bailey castle was built for Bertram de Bulmer by William the Conqueror for his support at Hastings, the mound of which can be seen to the south of the churchyard.

The extant remains of the stone castle at the western end of the village, completed in 1398, were built by John, Lord Neville, in the late-14th century. It fell into disrepair during the reign of King James I.

The Neville Castle was used by Richard III to house his nephew, Edward, Earl of Warwick, and his niece, Elizabeth of York.

The sheriff part of the place name comes from the fact that Ansketil and Bertram de Bulmer were both High Sheriffs of Yorkshire in 1115–28 and 1128–30 respectively.

In 1484 Richard, Duke of Gloucester, established the Council of the North, with its headquarters being at the castle. After 250 years the council relocated to York and so began the gradual decline, leaving the dramatic, atmospheric ruin we see today.

The Council of the North and the Pilgrimage of Grace

The Council of the North was an administrative body first set up in 1484 by Richard III to improve access to conciliar justice in the north of England. It was always in this part of England, first at Sheriff Hutton Castle and at Sandal Castle, and then at King's Manor, York. Henry VIII re-established the Council after the Reformation in 1537, when the north became identified with Roman Catholicism. It was abolished in 1641, just before the Civil War.

It was resistance to the Reformation that impelled Henry; resentment grew in the mainly Catholic north, culminating in a rebellion in York by a 30,000-strong Catholic army, carrying crosses and banners depicting the Holy Wounds. This became known as the Pilgrimage of Grace.

Henry promised that the rebels would be pardoned and a parliament would be held in York to discuss their demands. The rebels were convinced that monasteries would be reopened, and so went home. However, after the failed Roman Catholic, armed rebellion led by Sir Francis Bigod in Cumberland and Westmorland against Henry VIII, Henry had an excuse to arrest rebel leaders and to execute 200 of the people involved. Suppression followed. The council was reorganised again in 1538.

29

Margaret Clitherow: the Pearl of York

Pressing Saint Margaret, the Pearl of York.

Margaret Clitherow's humble but charming oratory is in the Shambles. She was the wife of John Clitherow, a butcher who lived here at number 35 (or possibly at number 10). Margaret was initially a Protestant but converted to Catholicism. During Elizabeth I's persecution of Catholics, Margaret was first jailed in 1577 for not attending church. She was jailed twice more at York Castle, the second time for 20 months. John had remained Protestant but helped her by paying her fines and tacitly accepting the refuge she gave to priests in their home.

Between 1582 and 1583, five priests were executed at Tyburn on Knavesmire and, when not in jail, Margaret would go at night to the gallows to visit the bodies. She was found guilty, in 1586, of 'harbouring and maintaining Jesuits and priests, enemies to the Queen's Majesty and her laws'. The usual penalty was hanging, but, due to her refusal to offer a plea at her trial at the city assizes in the Guildhall (called Common Hall at the time), she was sentenced to be pressed to death by Sir John Clenche (peine forte et dure) – having a door weighted with nearly half a ton of boulders placed on top of her at the tollbooth on Ouse Bridge. Within 15 minutes she was dead.

When she heard, Elizabeth I wrote to the citizens of York expressing her horror at the treatment meted out to a fellow woman. Margaret was beatified in 1929 and canonised in 1970 by Pope Paul VI, who described her as the 'Pearl of York'. Her embalmed hand is in the Bar Convent, and a church in Haxby near York is dedicated to her.

30

John Snow and Cholera

One of medical science's greatest discoveries

'A cholera patient experimenting with remedies,' coloured etching by Isaac Robert Cruikshank, c.1832 © Wellcome Collection. Isaac Robert Cruikshank (1789-1856), known as Robert Cruikshank, was the older brother of caricaturist and illustrator George Cruikshank. Random Shots #2

John Snow was born in 1813 in North Street, York. He relocated to Newcastle-upon-Tyne as an apprentice surgeon and then moved on to practice in Burnopfield, County Durham, and in Pateley Bridge before moving on as a student at the Hunteriasn School of Medicine in London's Great Windmill Street in 1836. Snow gained his memberships of the Royal College of Surgeons and then the Royal College Physicians. He was one of the pioneers of the dosage calculations of ether and chloroform as surgical anaesthetics, personally administering chloroform to Queen Victoria during the birth of her last child.

Snow called the 1854 cholera outbreak 'the most terrible outbreak of cholera which ever occurred in this kingdom'. He was working with the poor in Soho when he made one of medical science's greatest discoveries: he identified contaminated water as the pathway by which cholera was transmitted. Soho was a mess: filth was everywhere due to the large influx of people and the absence of proper sanitary services since the London sewer system had not reached them. Cowsheds, slaughter houses and grease-boiling dens lined the streets and contributed animal droppings, rotting garbage, infected fluids and other contaminants to the foul streets. Many cellars had cesspools swilling around underneath their floorboards, regularly replenished from the sewers and the excrement seeping in from the streets.

And so, it was decided to dump all this waste into the River Thames, polluting the water supply to unbelievable levels. Many of the victims, in 1854, were taken to the Middlesex Hospital, where their treatment was superintended by Florence Nightingale.

After the cholera flare up, which took 616 people, Snow dot-mapped the cases around the Broad Street (now Soho's Broadwick Street) pump and observed a cluster of cases there. To test this theory, he simply convinced the St James parish authorities to disable the pump by removing the handle: the number of cholera cases in the area fell immediately. Snow realised that the disease had nothing to do with miasma, it was, in fact, transmitted by germ-contaminated water. 'There was nothing in the air to account for the spread of cholera,' Snow said. Cholera was spread by persons ingesting a substance, not through atmospheric transmittal. He cited a case of two sailors, one with cholera and one without. Eventually the second became sick as well from 'accidentally' ingesting bodily fluids of the first. He also did a statistical analysis to illustrate the connection between the quality of the water source and cholera cases, demonstrating that water was being delivered to the outbreak area from the Thames, which was highly contaminated with visible and invisible products. The main culprits were the Southwark & Vauxhall Waterworks Company and the Lambeth Waterworks Company.

Snow's breakthrough helped bring the epidemic under control, although he, good scientist as he was, advised caution:

There is no doubt that the mortality was much diminished... by the flight of the population, which commenced soon after the outbreak; but the attacks had so far diminished before the use of the water was stopped,

> *that it is impossible to decide whether the well still contained the cholera poison in an active state, or whether, from some cause, the water had become free from it.*

Apparently, after the cholera epidemic had subsided, government officials put the Broad Street pump handle back on. They had responded only to the urgent threat posed to the population and afterwards they rejected Snow's theory. To accept his proposal would have meant indirectly accepting the oral-faecal method of transmission of disease, which they deemed too disgusting for most of the public to contemplate.

Cholera in York

The York cholera epidemic of 1832 affected at least 450 people and caused 185 deaths in a city population of 25,357. It arrived in June, lasted till the end of October, and was part of a pandemic — 'the Pestilence of India'. York was the 85th town to be hit in the country where, in total, cholera affected 431 towns and villages, infected 85,528 people and killed 31,376.

Graveyards in York were overrun, with St Cuthbert's, for example, experiencing a rise in the height of the ground as a result. The stench from shallow graves was insufferable. According to York Civic Trust:

> *In 1831 the epidemic made its first UK appearance in Sunderland. From there it seems to have travelled along rivers… York had ample notice of the likelihood of the disease's arrival when Leeds and Selby were affected and, following Privy Council advice, the city took clear precautions. Before its arrival, nine lectures on cholera were given by York's newly established Medical Society; the York Board of Health was reconvened; parish officers were instructed to inspect every house and to order, or to provide for, cleaning and whitewashing, and the removal of waste from privies, soil holes, ash heaps and urban pigsties. Some open sewers were covered over; special rates were raised for the Board of Health; and a house close to St George's churchyard was reserved for potential victims.*
>
> *None of that prevented Thomas Hughes, a hard-nosed waterman, from ferrying a party of vagrants, from Selby and elsewhere, across the River Ouse to York races on 28 May. Hughes, who lived in the notorious 'Hagworm's nest' just off Skeldergate, was the city's first cholera victim. The formal name of the 'nest' was Beedham Court. It had twice been the starting point for the city's much earlier outbreaks of plague. Five*

families shared a single privy; its cess pit was apt to flood the court; and a dunghill stood at its end. The dwellings were also damp and overcrowded. Before he fell ill, Hughes visited the Anchor Inn across the Ouse in Water Lane. The landlord died the next day, as did Hughes's neighbour, a sawyer, though Hughes himself seems to have recovered.

John Peacock Needham

John Peacock Needham was a lendal surgeon who preoccupied himself with the first cholera epidemic. When it ended in 1833, Needham worked hard to discover more about the disease and published his Facts & Observations Related to the *Disease Commonly Called Cholera as it has Recently Prevailed in the City of York.*

See:

Margaret C Barnet, 'The 1832 Cholera Epidemic in York', *Medical History,* vol.16, issue 1 Cambridge, 1972, 27-39.

Chrystal, Paul, *A History of the World in 100 Pandemics, Epidemics & Plagues,* Barnsley, 2021.

Durey, M, *The First Spasmodic Cholera Epidemic in York, 1832,* Borthwick Papers no. 46, York, 1974.

Halliday, S., Death and miasma in Victorian London: an obstinate belief. *British Medical Journal,* 323:1469–71, 2001.

Hempel, Sandra, *The Medical Detective: John Snow and the mystery of cholera,* London, 2006.

Snow, John, *On the mode of communication of cholera (2nd ed),* London, 1855.

Vinten-Johansen, Peter, *Cholera, Chloroform and the Science of Medicine: A life of John Snow,* Oxford, 2003.

31

The Resurrection Men, or Jerry Crunchers

Jerry Cruncher and Wife, Sol Eytinge.

One of eight illustrations for Dickens's A Tale of Two Cities and Great Expectations in the Ticknor & Fields (Boston), 1867, Diamond Edition.

Scanned image and text by Philip V. Allingham. Courtesy of the Victorian Web: https://victorianweb.org/art/illustration/eytinge/92.html

Instances of body snatching and burking (after Burke and Hare, where victims are murdered for their cadavers) abound in York – partly because the city was on the main coach route from London to Edinburgh with its famous medical school, a thriving market for cadavers. Even after the passing of the Anatomy Act in 1832, which legalised the trafficking of the bodies of lunatics and paupers between Poor Law Unions and medical schools, the 'unhallowed occupation' continued here – probably due to the opening of York's first medical school. The York Courant of 14 January 1834 reports that in St Saviourgate 'one Matthew Joy when questioned… stated that he merely wanted a skull for a person who had applied to him for one, in order to pulverise it, and mix it with some treacle, to give it to a person who was subject to fits.'

Jeremiah 'Jerry' Cruncher is a character in *Charles Dickens's 1859 A Tale of Two Cities.*

32

The Noel Terry Collection – Fairfax House

The dining room in Fairfax House.

The Noel Terry Collection can be seen in the various rooms of Fairfax House. It is 'An exceptional collection from the golden age of English cabinet-making and clock-making.'

Born in York in 1889, Noel Terry was chairman and great grandson of Joseph Terry, the founder of the global confectionery business, Terry's of York. The Fairfax House website tells us that over time Noel Terry amassed an 'outstanding collection of Georgian domestic furniture and clocks which Christie's have stated to be one of the best private collections of mid-eighteenth-century English furniture'. (www.fairfaxhouse.co.uk/fairfax-house/explore/noel-terry/)

The collection was originally housed at Goddards, Noel and Kathleen Terry's Arts and Crafts style-home on Tadcaster Road. The website continues:

> *Terry's tastes in collecting furniture were particular and surprisingly consistent, a dislike of gilding and anything too ornate, coupled with a demand for excellent quality. The collection, however, is not only significant because of its exceptional quality, but also because of its provenance. Indeed, its completeness as a collection (kept together in nearly its full entirety) helps to illustrate Terry's collecting passions, the development of his taste and the evolutions which took place in the process of collecting in the 20th century.*

A passionate lover of the city of his birth, in 1946 Terry was one of the four Founders of York Civic Trust. He insisted that the collection should remain 'for the benefit of the City of York'. After his death in 1979, his trustees offered the collection to the Civic Trust as a gift on the proviso that it was placed on permanent display.

See:

Webb, Gerry (2001), *Fairfax of York: The Life and History of a Noble Family*, York

33

Lancelot Blackburne

Archbishop, spy and Pirate

Portrait of Lancelot Blackburne (1658–1743), Archbishop of York, attributed to Joseph Highmore (1692-1780); Christ Church, Oxford.

Lancelot Blackburne (1658–1743) was Archbishop of York from 1724 until his death, before which a record of 1681 reveals that he was paid £20 (£3,335 in 2021) by Charles II for 'secret services', and spent time as a pirate on Nevis in the Caribbean in the 1680s. In 1724 he became Archbishop of York. Neglecting his duties generally, the *Dictionary of National Biography* records 'his reputation for carnality' and 'the laxity of his moral precepts,' while *Brewer's Rogues, Villains and Eccentrics* elegantly comments that '[his] behaviour was seldom of a standard to be expected of an archbishop. In many respects, his behaviour was seldom of a standard to be expected of a pirate.' He was famously ejected by John Disney, the vicar of St Mary's Church, Nottingham, after a confirmation service during which he asked for his pipe, tobacco and ale. One local legend in York has it that Dick Turpin was his butler.

34

George Frederick Sitwell

The Sitwells – 'a knockabout nepotistic band'

The opulent interior of Bootham Park Hospital in 1993, formerly York Lunatic Asylum, belies the atrocities that were committed there in the 19th century. (Courtesy of York Press)

George Frederick Sitwell (1828–83) attained the rank of Captain in the 1st Life Guards, 85th Shropshire Light Infantry and 3rd Light Dragoons. The later Sitwells are famous for the literary clique which Edith, Osbert and Sacheverell formed and which, some say, rivalled the Bloomsbury Group in the period 1916 to 1930.

It is, however, Captain Fred who interests us. He was one of the most eccentric members of a decidedly eccentric family and became increasingly mad. In the 1860s, he was committed to York Lunatic Asylum where he ended his days. The literary critic FR Leavis asserted that 'the Sitwells belong to the history of publicity rather than literature'. Roger Lewis (*The Times,* 18 July 2015) remarked 'to my mind, Edith (1887–1964), Osbert (1892–1969) and Sacheverell (1897–1988) are what we had instead of the Marx Brothers – a knockabout nepotistic band.'

Their principal seat, Renishaw Hall, built in 1626 in the north of Derbyshire, six miles from Chesterfield and Sheffield, was the common factor for the family. They struck gold when iron ore was found under their garden in the 1630s and set about churning out nails and screws, an industry conveniently bolstered by the demand created by the Civil War and the army's need for iron weapons. Wood for the charcoal, to feed the furnaces, came from the family estates.

Many of the male Sitwells were called George or Francis, or both; to ring the changes in the latter part of the 18th century one infant was named Sitwell Sitwell. He became MP for the rotten borough of West Looe in Cornwall, a place he never visited. Sitwell Sitwell died age 42 of 'gout in the head'. Tenant farmers' rents bought in yet more money (about £22,000 pa), which fuelled continuous home improvements including a ballroom for a ball attended by the Prince Regent.

Family correspondence reveals that in the mid-18th century the various Sitwells enjoyed York. Autumn 1735 saw Francis Sitwell saying of his cousins that they are at York where 'abundance of our neighbouring gentry have took into their heads to rendezvous this winter, where they find good and cheap provisions, and operas, plays, musick meetings, and I know not what.' We hear of him later subscribing to the York Assemblies and the Sheffield Assemblies. In the winter of 1773 he rented a house near Bootham Bar, handy for the Assembly Rooms. No light traveller was Francis – he brought all his furniture with him. His wife, Mary Warneford, was 'the beauty of Bath', a bluestocking or précieuse who shared his love of music. Her father was a canon of York.

Meanwhile, Captain Fred started calling himself the Duke of Renshaw and stopped washing, which may have been the last straw prompting his confinement to York Asylum. Other Sitwells died of smallpox or drowned. The family, like other aristocrats, had its share of drunks, womanisers and bigamists. As with other aristocratic families, bankruptcy loomed in 1849, and the opulent contents of Renishaw were sold off. By another stroke of geological good fortune, in 1870 a seam of black gold, coal, was discovered, again under the garden – the garden which just continued to give – and the house contents were bought back and restored lock, stock and barrel to Renishaw again.

Sir George Sitwell, 4th baronet (b. 1860), provided some stability and fathered Edith, Osbert and Sachie. One of George's claims to fame was, while at Oxford, he exposed the famous and controversial medium Mrs Florence Eliza Cook as a fraud, 'seizing hold of her during a "séance" at the British National Association of Spiritualists' in 1880, and revealed that the medium was not in her chair – a feat which he saw significant enough to include in his Who's Who entry. In 1883 he attended, uninvited, the coronation of Alexander III in the Kremlin, dressed up as a Yorkshire Dragoon.

Osbert tells us that Sir George invented a musical toothbrush and a 'miniature revolver for shooting wasps'. In southern Italy he would dine in verminous trattoria decked out in full white tie and tails. On returning to Derbyshire he set about recreating a Mediterranean landscape using unemployed fisermen for labour (in landlocked Derbyshire). His dipsomaniac and spendthrift wife, Ida, did time in 1915 for fraud, having had her daughter pawn her mother's false teeth to buy a bottle of whisky. On her release she bought a pig at a Conservative Association bazaar in Scarborough, convinced that it was 'able to foretell the future'.

Osbert fought bravely in the trenches despite claims he wore lace pyjamas. Sachie married Georgia Doble in 1929; she was 'Oswald Mosley's main mistress'.

See:

Bradford, Sarah, *The Sitwells,* Sarah Bradford, published in 1996 by the National Portrait Gallery to accompany the exhibition 'The Sitwells and the arts of the 1920s and 1930s'.

Seward, Desmond, *Renishaw Hall: The Story of the Sitwells, Elliott & Thompson,* 2015.

Lehmann, John, *A Nest of Tigers: The Sitwells in Their Times,* 1968.

35

Mary Ward

Imprisoned in Munich for heresy

A cloister of nuns at the Bar Convent in about 1900.

Mary Ward (d. 1645) is celebrated in the museum that is an integral part of the Bar Convent and is buried in St Thomas's in Osbaldwick. She founded the Institute of the Blessed Virgin Mary, opening schools in Flanders before the Institute was suppressed by the Pope. After imprisonment in Munich for heresy, she returned to England and re-established the Institute in Heworth in 1644. The 50 pictures climbing the Bar Convent staircase depict her life; they are reproduced from 17th-century paintings from the house of the Institute of Augsburg. The 2,000 or so books in the library date from between

1508 and 1850 and, unlike some library collections, are well used, obviously read, and annotated. The convent also retains a relic of the hand of St Margaret Clitherow. In 1977 the day school and boarding school here merged to become the Bar Convent Grammar School, when boys were admitted for the first time; in 1985 it became part of All Saints Catholic School.

Mary Ward

See:

Wallace, David (2012). 'Holy Amazon: Mary Ward of Yorkshire, 1585-1645', *Strong Women: Life, Text, and Territory 1347-1645,* Oxford.

Wallace, David (2006). 'Periodizing Women: Mary Ward (1585-1645) and the Premodern Canon', Journal of Medieval and Early Modern Studies, 36 (2), pp. 397–453.

Lux-Sterritt, L and Mangion C (eds), 'Mary Ward's English Institute and Prescribed Female Roles in the Early Modern Church"', *Gender, Catholicism and Spirituality: Women and the Roman Catholic Church in Britain and Europe, 1200-1900,* Basingstoke.

36

Charles Dickens, Richard Chicken and Stonewall Jackson

'The deep organ's bursting heart throb through the shivering air'

The breath-taking Five Sisters Window in York Minster.

On one of his visits to York in 1838, Dickens describes in his *Letters* a visit to his friend, John Camidge, organist at the Minster, who showed him around. Dickens was particularly struck by 'the deep organ's bursting heart throb through the shivering air' and the Five Sisters Window. Dickens's story about the window appears in Nicholas *Nickleby* as the *Five Sisters of York.* The first reading of the book was given in York at the long-gone Festival Concert Rooms in Blake Street; the *Yorkshire Gazette* tells us that Dickens 'elicited unbounded applause and sent his audience home delighted'. Mr Wilkins Micawber from *David Copperfield,* too, finds his origins in York, based as he is on Richard Chicken.

Richard Chicken (1799-1866) – the feckless and eccentric Mr Micawber

Charles Dickens's model for Mr Micawber was Richard Chicken, a feckless and eccentric character who, in 1847, worked in the same railway office as Alfred Lamert Dickens (1822–60), Charles's railway engineer brother. Alfred Dickens was resident engineer for the York and North Midland Railway at the firm of John Cass Burkinshaw at 29 (now 71) Micklegate. Charles would have visited Alfred and met his colleagues.

Chicken was baptised in St Michael's Spurriergate in August 1799. After schooling at Bingley Grammar School, he was given a clerkship at the York Ecclesiastical Court. Unsuited to the necessary meticulous detail required in this work, he became an unsuccessful actor in York and Nottingham, after which he established himself as master at the Swan Street School in Clementhorpe. He later lived at 26 St Mary's Row (later Victor Street) opposite the Golden Ball in Bishophill. Between them, he and his wife Louisa had 12 children, seven of whom died in childhood. Chicken at one time was self-styled Professor of Elocution and Lecturer on Defective Annunciation. He died in the Huntington Union Workhouse.

Stonewall Jackson – a rare Presbyterian

Thomas Jonathan 'Stonewall' Jackson (d. 1863), Confederate General in the American Civil War, visited York in the 1830s. *The Times* reported in his obituary: 'He dwelt with great animation upon the vibration of the air produced by the deep notes of the organ in York Minster... it is rare to find in a Presbyterian such appreciation and admiration of Cathedral magnificence.'

37

The Rowntree Exploding Bananas

A dilapidated part of the Nestlé (formerly Rowntree) building on Haxby Road, now converted into apartments.

T*he Cocoa Works Magazine,* or CWM, to give it its official name, was launched in March 1902. The last issue was published in May 1986. Over those 84 years, it provides a fascinating and detailed record of life at Rowntree. Its subtitle was *A Journal in the Interest of the Employees of Rowntree & Co Ltd, York;* its aims and scope, in up to 40 pages per issue (although this was severely reduced during the paper shortages of the two World Wars), was to provide a means of communication within the company to keep everyone informed about what was going on at all levels. *CWM* was seen as one way in which the company could make good the loss of that personal touch when Joseph Rowntree had to remove himself from his treasured daily contact with his workers.

The inaugural issue of *The Cocoa Works Magazine* in 1902 featured John Wilhelm's account of the explosion on board the Royal Mail Steamer Para, which would have been comical were it not so tragic; he and Constance had the misfortune to be on the vessel which was bringing, amongst other cargoes, Rowntree cocoa back from Trinidad and Granada:

> *there was an appalling roar… a momentary flash followed by blinding darkness. Mrs R and myself found ourselves hurled into the air... ships officers and crew behaved as Englishmen should... the captain, while in the air, shouted for the Fire Brigade.*

The explosion was caused by a shipment of bananas; one of the passengers was attempting to see if, by extracting oxygen from the containers holding his bananas, deterioration of the fruit could be avoided or retarded. Bananas were increasingly popular at the time, with five million bunches imported into the UK in 1904, up from two million in 1900. The result of the explosion was catastrophic, with three dead and others injured, one of whom was 'in delirium'.

See:

Chrystal, Paul, 'Rowntree Tales', in Stephen W. Angell, *Quakers, Business, and Industry: Quakers and the Disciplines: Volume 4,* 2017.

Chrystal, Paul, *The Rowntree family of York,* 2013.

Chrystal, Paul, *Rowntree, The Early Years, Barnsley,* 2021.

https://www.rowntreesociety.org.uk/wp-content/uploads/2018/10/Exhibition-Book.pdf

38

The York Army Museum

The funeral sword of Captain Sir Tom Moore

York Army Museum Zone One tank

The York Army Museum tells the story of regiments that have been raised in or are associated with Yorkshire from 1685 to the present day.

The focus is, therefore, on the Royal Dragoon Guards collection and the Yorkshire Regiment collection – one cavalry, one infantry. Each of these regiments can trace their history back over 300 years. The museum can also offer exhibits showcasing their antecedents:

- the 4th Royal Irish Dragoon Guards, the 5th (Princess Charlotte of Wales's) Dragoon Guards, the 6th (Inniskilling) Dragoons, the 7th (The Princess Royal's) Dragoon Guards, the 5th Royal Inniskilling Dragoon Guards and the 4th/7th Royal Dragoon Guards.

Captain Tom Moore's sword.

- the East Yorkshire Regiment (Duke of York's Own), the West Yorkshire Regiment (Prince of Wales's Own) and the Prince of Wales's Own Regiment of Yorkshire.

The museum is privileged to be able to display the funeral sword of Captain Sir Tom Moore, which has been donated to the museum.

It is accommodated in a building called the Drill Hall, formerly the HQ for the 1st East Riding of Yorkshire Artillery Volunteers from 1885. The museum was opened in the 1980s.

39

The Jewish Massacre of 1190

The Jewish settlement at York is still 'the most famous of all the provincial Jewries of medieval England'

- Robert Davies, The Medieval Jews of York (1874)

Clifford's Tower, spring 2023.

The memorial tablet.

This atrocity against the Jews took place on 16 March 1190, when a rioting mob of townsfolk forced the Jews in York to take refuge in Clifford's Tower, which was under the control of the sheriff. The castle was torched and the Jews were massacred. The chronicler William of Newburgh described the rioters as acting 'without any scruple of Christian conscientiousness' in wiping out the Jewish community.

Anti-semitic feeling was running high in 12th-century England, inflamed by Christian zeal that in turn was stoked by the Crusades. This focused aggression against Jews across England, France and Germany, as well as against Muslims in the Holy Land. Richard I was soon to set off on Crusade himself. Rioting spread throughout England when prominent Jews, including Benedict of York, had been denied entry to Richard I's coronation banquet in 1189. Benedict, of Spen Lane, was the wealthiest Jew in York and was killed in the rioting at Westminster after he and Jocen of Coney Street gate-crashed the coronation despite a ban on Jews attending.

The New Jewish Encyclopaedia tells us that the Crusades were a 'bitter and prolonged ordeal' for the Jews of Europe; mobs were incited by the leaders of the Crusades to pillage and wipe out whole Jewish communities, rallying to such odious cries as 'Before attempting to revenge ourselves upon the Moslem unbelievers, let us first revenge ourselves upon the killers of Christ living in our midst!' Thousands of Jews died, and entire Jewish communities were massacred. To this day, the Jewish liturgy contains prayers commemorating the martyrs of those dark years.

In York, the first mention of Jewry is by Betram de Bulmer, Sheriff of York, who records the death of a Jew in 1130. By 1290 there was something like 2,000 to 3,000 in England. Persecution of the Jews did not start at Clifford's Tower: one Saxon Archbishop of York prohibited his flock from eating or doing business with Jews; a law under Edward the Confessor describes them as 'the King's chattels'. Generally, the church regarded them as 'the accursed people', blaming them for the execution of Christ. Jews could not hold public office as this entailed the taking of a Christian oath; they could not hold land because feudal tenure entailed Christian fealty; they were excluded from much commerce on account of the exclusive York guilds. Such racist and punitive restrictions did not end with the Jews; many years later Quakers in York were punished with similar restrictions. For the Jewish that only really left money-lending: also, no one else could lend money because the Christian church forbade usury. Jews, then, were seen as a necessary evil. Ironically, Aaron of Lincoln financed nine Yorkshire Cistercian monasteries with Jewish money, which was repaid with interest.

Rioting spread from Norwich, Stamford and Lincoln to York, where, in March 1190, thugs broke into the house of the late Benedict of York, killing his widow and children, setting the house on fire, and looting Benedict's treasure. The Jews had protection from the king and sought asylum in the royal castle, barricading themselves into the wooden keep. Many rioters saw the unrest as an opportunity to wipe out the substantial debts they owed to Jewish money-lenders in the city; they had borrowed heavily but had failed in their attempts to secure lucrative royal appointments and so could not afford to repay their debts without the loans. Indeed, after the massacre they burned all records of their debts held in the Minster, so absolving themselves from repayment.

The Jews in the keep locked out the royal constable, who then ordered the castle be taken by force by knights with siege engines. A hermit who had been inciting the mob was killed by a falling stone, which only incensed the mob yet further. Most of the Jews chose to commit suicide: the only other option was to renounce their faith and surrender to forced baptism or death at the hands of the rioters. The Jews were led by the wealthy Jew Josce and Rabbi Yomtob, a scholar, who had come to York from Joigny in France. After killing their wives and children they set fire to the wooden keep and they themselves died in the flames. It was Rabbi Yomtob who encouraged his fellow Jews to commit suicide during the massacre, and Yomtob himself killed 60 of his comrades once they had killed their own wives and children.

The massacre was seen as an insult to the dignity and authority of King Richard, and a royal inquest was held soon afterwards that resulted in a heavy fine on the city. No individuals were ever punished for the atrocity on that horrific night. The Jewish community in York did recover after the massacre and a Jewish presence remained in York until the expulsion of Jews from England in 1290. However, the massacre only led to more persecution, with Jews ordered to wear a yellow badge, indicative of the myth that they murdered Christian children on the Passover. Sadly, this was not to be the last time yellow badges marked out Jewish people from the crowd. Punitive laws, restrictive bureaucracy, a ban on having Christian servants and healing the sick and accusations of wholesale coin clipping all conspired to make the life of a Jew in

England as wretched as possible. In 1290 Edward I expelled all 16,000 of England's Jews; many of them either, , robbed or thrown into the sea in their efforts to reach the continent.

We can assume from Archbishop Egbert's ruling around 750 CE that all priests were to ring their bells at the proper time, day and night, and that the now familiar sound of bells tolling in York Minster stems from at least the mid-8th century. There was, however, a pause in the aftermath of the Jewish massacre when the Bishop of Ely, on behalf of William I, ordered that the bells remain silent until the arrogant clergy came and made appropriate submission at his feet.

As postscript, 31 October 1978 was a significant day in York – it was the day when a memorial tablet was finally unveiled by the Archbishop of York and the Chief Rabbi of England at the foot of Clifford's Tower to remember the Jews burnt and slaughtered there.

See:

Maier, Christoph T. (2022), Church, Stephen D. (ed.), *"Crusaders and Jews: The York Massacre of 1190 Revisited"*, Anglo-Norman Studies XLIV: Proceedings of the Battle Conference 2021

York *1190: Jews and Others in the Wake of Massacre.* University of York - Centre for Medieval Studies. March 2010

The York Massacre, as Described by Ephraim of Bonn". Jewish Virtual Library

Abulafia, Anna Sapir (16 October 2014). *"William of Newburgh on the attack on the Jews of York in 1190"*. Jewish/non-Jewish Relations

40

The Kohima Museum

Kukri and Japanese boots in the museum.

The hugely decisive Battle of Kohima in north-east India, close to its border with Burma, took place between 4 April and 22 June 1944 and marked the limit of the Japanese Army advance into India. Here the enemy was stopped, defeated and forced into retreat. The Japanese invasion of India was halted at Kohima.

The Kohima Museum, Imphal Barracks, Fulford Road, commemorates the actions of the British 2nd Division from 1942–46, focusing on the Siege and Battle of Kohima. It exhibits a vast selection of memorabilia from the event, including war diaries, uniforms, medals, maps, charts, ground photographs and weapons.

Kohima, a hill town in Nagaland, 5,000 feet (1,500 metres) above sea level in the middle of the Naga Hills, was the location of one of the most bitterly fought battles of the Second World War. The Kohima Reunion has taken place annually in York to commemorate the battle. Kohima involved the best parts of three Divisions: 31st Japanese Division, 2nd British Division and Brigades from 5th and 7th Indian Divisions. The fighting went on for 64 days over impossibly difficult terrain in monsoon conditions and involved numerous Regiments fighting different actions simultaneously.

See:

Chrystal, Paul, *Gunners from the Sky, The 1st Airlanding Light Regiment R.A in Italy and at the Battle of Arnhem,* Barnsley, 2023.

Chrystal, Paul, *The Seaforth Highlanders, Aiding the King 1881 to 1961*, Barnsley, 2023.

Chrystal, Paul, *From the Northwest Frontier to Stalag 383: The Experiences of a Seaforth Highlander in World War II*, Barnsley, 2023.

41

The Dettingen Standard

He [Richardson] was to suffer some 37 wounds, from sword cuts and thrusts and flying bullets

The standard is made from crimson silk damask and its two sides are now mounted separately on boards.

At Dettingen (now Karlstein-am-Main), Germany, the combined Allied Armies, known as the Pragmatic Army and under the command of King George II, encountered a strong French force under the Duc de Noiailles. The regiment website explains how:

Somewhere in the middle of this uncoordinated and furious melée was Cornet Henry Richardson of Ligonier's Horse, carrying with him the 'First', or Colonel's, Standard of the Regiment. The standard, the point around which the Regiment rallied and to which it looked for cohesion, the means by which the commanders of the Army might know where the Regiment was, and the symbolic representation of the Regiment's honour, was naturally a prime target for enemy attention. The bearer, with one hand grasping the staff and the other controlling his horse, was virtually defenceless. The Standard bearer thus was given an escort, then as today, of two Warrant Officers or Senior Non-Commissioned Officers, who flanked him wherever he went. However, it was Richardson who was to earn the fame and renown for that day; his escort were probably just as valorous as he himself, but it is his name that has ever since been revered in the Regiment. In defending the Standard, he was to suffer some thirty-seven wounds, from sword cuts and thrusts and flying bullets.

Now in the York Army Museum, the Dettingen Standard is made from crimson silk damask. It remains, to this day, the oldest British Cavalry Standard in existence, a colourful and silent testament to the valour and determination of Cornet Henry Richardson and Ligonier's Horse.

Also housed in the Museum, opposite the Standard, and taken from the battlefield of Dettingen on that same day, stands one of the pair of Dettingen Drums; two kettledrums taken from the French cavalry during the battle, and kept ever since.

Obverse of a standard carried at the Battle of Dettingen (27 June 1743) by the 8th Regiment of Horse, the regiment of which Major General John Ligonier (1680–1770) was colonel (later the 7th Dragoon Guards and now part of the Royal Dragoon Guards).

42

The bizarre marriage of Arthur Munby and Hannah Cullwick

Portrait of Hannah Cullwick dressed up as maidservant in 1860 (Trinity College Library, Cambridge, Arthur Munby collection).

Arthur Joseph Munby (1828–1910) was a man of many and considerable talents, including diarist, poet, portrait photographer, barrister and solicitor. Historian Leonore Davidoff writes that Arthur Munby's relationship with Hannah Cullwick was predicated on redefining the established sexual and social norms of Victorian Britain. Their relationship also challenged the social boundaries surrounding race and empire by engaging via Cullwick's

A true slave to love.

racial crossdressing. The transgressions of sexuality in the public and private spheres, and the mixing of different socio-economic demographics, allowed Munby and Cullwick an opportunity to actively challenge and exercise control over the rigid norms of Victorian society.

On Thursday, 1 March 1827 23-year-old lawyer Joseph Munby, Arthur's father, had married Caroline Eleanor Forth, three years his junior, at St Helen's church at the end of Stonegate. The usually buzzing River Ouse was paralysed by ice, 'the great accumulation of ice in the river'. The couple went to live in The Terrace in Clifton in the north of York; they raised seven children. Caroline's uncle was James Woodhouse, three times Mayor of York; Joseph's solicitor father served as Under-Sheriff of York. The Munbys clearly enjoyed Clifton:

> *There is a... pleasant place of entertainment called the Marquee Gardens... to which parties resort in large numbers during the summer season... a more retired and pleasant entertainment cannot be found within so short a distance from the City of York.*

The Munby family are well-known as one of the oldest names in the legal profession in York – they ran the long-established firm of Munby & Scott in York. The firm of Munby Solicitors was at 9 St Helen's Square from *c.*1830–1838. In 1838 the firm moved to 4 Blake Street, where it remained until 2007 when the building was sold and the firm merged with Langleys. In 1838 the family moved to 3 Blake Street, next door to the office. From 1848, the Munby family lived at Clifton Holme (at the end of Ousecliffe Gardens, now St Hilda's Garth) in a new-build grand residence.

Joseph Munby was an extremely active professional, always at the centre of York life. Apart from establishing and running a prominent legal firm, he was Clerk to the Magistrates in 1836 and Clerk to the County Gaol Sessions and Clerk to the Visiting Justices in 1845. Additionally, he was a founder of the York School for the Blind in King's Court; Secretary to the York County Hospital, on the committee of York's Bluecoat School and York School of Art, a friend of York Ragged Schools and the Yorkshire Philosophical Society.

Arthur was the eldest of the five children, born in York in Clifton and baptised in September 1828 in St Olave's Church. Arthur Munby attended St Peter's School, then located in Minster Yard. The school amalgamated with the Proprietary School in Clifton and Arthur followed it there in 1844, and then on to Trinity College, Cambridge, two years later, where he studied classics, theology and mathematics. He was called to the Bar from Lincoln's Inn in 1855 and worked as a civil servant in the Ecclesiastical Commissioners' office from 1858 until his retirement in 1888. His published poetry included *Benoni* (1852) and *Verses New and Old* (1865). He taught Latin at the Working Men's College for more than a decade and helped promote the Working Men's College Volunteer Corp (WMCVC), a response to the national call for Volunteer Rifle Corps (1859) to defend against a perceived war threat from Napoleon III. Munby wrote verses of support, the *Invicta: a Song of 1860*, for the 19th Middlesex Regiment, a regiment to which the WMCVC was attached. In 1864, a sister Working Women's College was established; Munby was a leading spirit of, and teacher at, the new college.

Munby's poetry is characterised by its absolute sincerity, its scholarship, its technical skill, its descriptive power, and its keen feeling for and close observation of nature and rural life. Outside this, his dominant note may be said to have been what has been called 'the glorification of the working woman,' with especial insistence on the dignity of manual labour.

https://victorianweb.org/authors/munby/bio.html

So, Munby had a passionate, scholarly interest in working-class women, especially those who performed hard physical labour. He often spent his time wandering the streets of London and other industrial cities where he questioned working women enquiring about their lives and details of their work, while noting their clothes and dialects. The observations were recorded in his journals. These journals reflect his desire for the strength and care of a working woman. He was also an amateur artist – his diaries feature sketches of working women. He collected hundreds of photographs, including women who laboured in collieries, kitchen maids, milkmaids, charwomen and acrobats. His diaries and images give us extensive historical information on the lives of working-class Victorian women, and our social history of the period is much enriched as a result. Much of his findings can be found in his final book, *Faithful Servants: being epitaphs and obituaries recording their names and services* (1891).

He noted in 1861 that on London Bridge:

> *One meets them [working women] at every step: young women carrying large bundles of umbrella frames home to be covered; young women carrying cages full of hats, which yet want the silk and the binding; coster girls often dirty and sordid, going to fill their empty baskets, and above all female sackmakers.*

As for Hannah Cullwick, Munby was taken by her size (5ft 71/2in, 161 lbs) and strength, combined with the nobility of character he claimed to see in working women. Cullwick saw him as an idealised gentlemen who celebrated the intense labour she did as a maid of all work.

Cullwick was proud to call herself Munby's 'drudge and slave', and called him 'Massa', in a Master/slave relationship. Most of the time she wore a leather strap around her right wrist and a locking chain around her neck, to which Munby had a key. She wrote letters almost daily to him, detailing her long hours of work. She would arrange to visit him 'in [her] dirt', parading the results of a full day's cleaning and other domestic work. She had a particular interest in Munby's boots, cleaning hundreds each year, sometimes by licking them. She once told Munby that she could tell where her 'Massa' had been by how his boots tasted.

Hannah Cullwick's diaries reveal that her erotic games with Munby often included infantilism and ageplay, with Cullwick carrying Munby in her arms and holding him on her lap.

On 9 July 1909 she died, aged 76; the cause of death was recorded as 'failure of heart action and senile decay'. Her remains were buried in St Andrew's churchyard in Shifnal, near Telford and her gravestone bears the words 'she was for 36 years of pure and unbroken love the wedded wife of Arthur Munby of Clifton Holme in the Wapentake of Bulmer [near York]'.

Munby died in January 1910, aged 81. He left an estate of £26,000. He bequeathed his books and two deed-boxes filled with correspondence, diaries, and photographs, to the British Museum. They were unable to accept this legacy, and provision was made for the items to be kept at Trinity College, Cambridge, and not opened until 1950.

See:

Atkinson, Diane, Love *and Dirt: The Marriage of Arthur Munby and Hannah Cullwick*, New York, 2002.

Chrystal, Paul, *Factory Girls: The Working Lives of Women & Children*, Barnsley, 2022.

Davidoff, Leonore, 1979, 'Class and Gender in Victorian England: The Diaries of Arthur J. Munby and Hannah Cullwick'. *Feminist Studies*. 5 (1): 87–141.

Hudson, Derek, *Munby: Man of Two Worlds: The Life and Diaries of Arthur J. Munby*, 1828–1910, London, 1974.

Reay, Barry, *Watching Hannah: Sexuality, Horror and Bodily De-formation in Victorian England*, Reaktion, 2002.

Stanley, Liz (ed.), *The Diaries of Hannah Cullwick, Victorian Maidservant*, Rutgers, 1984.

Wills, Matthew , 'The Bizarre Victorian Diaries of Cullwick and Munby', *JSTOR Daily*, 10 September 2018.

www.casebook.org/dissertations/rip-munby.html

https://archives.exploreyork.org.uk/index.php/munby-family

www.findadeathforum.com/showthread.php?24854-Hannah-Culwick-Victorian-Maid-led-amazing-life

43

The Mansion House and the Sigismund Sword

The website introduces this treasure as:
Past the grandeur of the prominent green doors and beautiful facade lies a home built for entertaining royalty, with a rich civic and personal history. As the oldest purpose-built home for a Lord Mayor in the country, the stories of scandal and frivolity woven into the fabric of the building are still being told …' (www.mansionhouseyork.com)

Detail from the scabbard of Sigismund Sword at the Mansion House, York, showing the 'scorpions' or 'dragons'.

Built on the site of the chapel and kitchens of St Christopher's Hall, Mansion House is the official residence of the Right Honourable the Lord Mayor of York during his or her year in office. York had a house for its Lord Mayor 20 years before London's Mansion House.

York's Mansion House is based on the Queen's Gallery at Somerset House in London, which was designed by Inigo Jones and built between 1723 and 1733 on the site of the chapel of the Guild of St Christopher. It houses the York Civic Plate and Insignia – notably the sword of the Emperor Sigismund, which originally hung over his stall as Knight of the Garter in St George's Chapel, Windsor, and was given to York in 1439. Sigismund was King of Hungary and Croatia from 1387 to 1437, and Holy Roman Emperor from 1433 to 1437. Today the sword is used on ceremonial occasions such as freedom of the city, Mayor Making and Full council. The sword was also used for the State visit in 2012, which saw Queen Elizabeth II presented with the Sigismund sword before entering the city at Micklegate Bar. She was greeted at the Bar by the sword-bearer who, partially unsheathing the sword, presented it to her; she touched the blade and was permitted to enter. On 9 November 2022, King Charles III and Camilla, Queen consort, soon after their elevation, followed tradition and entered at Micklegate with the same ceremony.

Apart from Edward VI, Queen Mary I and Queen Elizabeth I, all the rulers of England from Richard II to Charles I visited York at least once. Richard II came to York nine times.

The Mansion House is famously threatened with being burnt to the ground in Gaskell's *Sylvia's Lovers* (1863), if the Mayor, in 1777, failed to satisfy the demands of the press-gang. The architect remains a mystery. It may have been William Etty. Doncaster has the only other Mansion House outside York and London.

See:

Kightly, Charles, *Lords of the City, The Lord Mayors and their Mansion House*, York, 1980.

Pevsner, Nikolaus, *The Buildings of England, Yorkshire: York and the East Riding*, London, 1995.

44

The Minster Astronomical Clock

World War Two pilot navigation system

The Astronomical Clock.

From 1750 until 1871, the south entrance to the Minster was surmounted by a splendid clock. This was installed in 1750 by Henry Hindley to replace a ramshackle mediaeval clock. Henry Hindley's Striking Clock was moved to the North Transept, where it features two carved oak figures or 'Quarter Jacks' who strike the hours and quarters with their rods.

As famous today is the astronomical clock installed in the Minster in 1955, as a memorial to the Yorkshire-based Allied aircrew who flew from bases in Yorkshire and the North-East and who died during World War Two. One face shows the precise position of the sun in relation to the Minster at any given time, while the other gives the position of the northern stars by which aircrew would have navigated.

45

Robert Aske

A rotting example to us all

(Newly restored in 2022) Clifford's Tower; the site of Aske's execution.

Aske was one of the leaders of the Pilgrimage of Grace, who, in 1537, was executed in York for treason related to his opposition to the Suppression of Religious Houses Act 1535 in 1536. His corpse was then taken to a local blacksmith in Pavement where it was riveted through with chains and then hung from a 35ft gibbet.

It was still there, somewhat wasted, when Henry visited the city in 1541, a stark and putrefying warning to other potential traitors.

The Pilgimage was a popular, badly orchestrated, uprising in the autumn of 1536 in protest against Henry VIII's break with the Catholic Church, the Dissolution of the Monasteries, and the policies of Thomas Cromwell. Initially Aske had nothing to do with the rebellion, but he took up the rebel cause. By 10 October 1536, he had come to be regarded as their 'chief captain'. Most of Yorkshire, and parts of Northumberland, Durham, Cumberland, and Westmorland, were in revolt.

Nine thousand insurgents marched on York, where Aske arranged for the expelled monks and nuns to return to their houses; the King's tenants were driven out and religious observance resumed.

The jury that condemned Aske as a traitor included his brother John. Others suffered a similar fate, not least two Carthusian monks from Hull who were left to rot to bits outside the city walls in chains.

See:

Gasquet, Francis Aidan, *Henry VIII and the English Monasteries*, G. Bell, 1906.

Burton, Edwin. 'Pilgrimage of Grace', *The Catholic Encyclopaedia* Vol. 12, New York, Robert Appleton Company, 1911.

Shahan, Thomas, 'Robert Aske', *The Catholic Encyclopaedia* Vol. 1., New York, 1907.

46

York Castle Museum

Welcome to a former women's prison

The former women's prison in the Castle Museum.

York Castle Museum opened in 1938 and is one of Britain's leading museums showcasing everyday life. It is famous for its Victorian street, Kirkgate, named after the museum's founder, Dr John Lamplugh Kirk, a Pickering doctor who collected everyday objects, his 'bygones', and for whom the museum was converted from the Women's Prison as somewhere to keep them safe for future generations.

The shops you'll find on our Victorian street Kirkgate are genuine examples from the period. Much research has been done into their history to ensure that both the facades and their interiors are as authentic as possible.

Dick Turpin's grave is nearby in the garden on the site of St George's Church. He was executed on 7 April 1739, after spending time in a cell, which can still be seen in the Debtor's Prison in the museum.

Highlights include:

Shaping the body: 400 years of fashion, food and life

Senior curator of history Ali Bodley tells us an iron corset, crotchless pantaloons from the time of Jane Austen, bum rolls and a killer dress are a few of the items featured in the latest permanent exhibition which charts the way fashion, food and fitness have shaped the body over the last 400 years.

Mechanical marvels

Fourteen weird and wonderful 20th century machines are now on display across the museum for people of all ages to find, play with and enjoy! These amazing machines include Automata, Mutoscopes, and a Stereoscope, and depict stories of Dracula, Aladdin, Sooty and many more.

Toy stories

Go back to your childhood and rediscover some of your favourite toys: bikes, bath toys, computer games, Lego and beautiful handmade dolls are among the toys on show from the last 150 years. Pure nostalgia. Children will be fascinated by these classics.

The sixties

The museum website reveals how 'The Sixties' exhibition 'aims to recreate the spirit of this exciting decade, which saw momentous change in so many areas of public and private life'. More nostalgia.

The gallery uses fascinating and iconic objects from our social history, art, fashion, military and astronomy collections to recreate the atmosphere of change that swept over the country during the 1960s. Highlights include a Lambretta scooter, a Dansette record player, The Beatles records and fashion by Mary Quant. It explores key themes such as fashion, music, the home, sport, childhood, the space race, free love, counterculture and women's liberation.

Raindale Mill – Mill on the Foss

An early 19th-century flour mill removed from Raindale, Newton, on the North York Moors, to the grounds of the York Castle Museum in 1965.

47

The Roman Bath Museum

Step back into the Roman occupation of York

This fascinating and unique museum, hidden away next to the Royal Bath pub in St Helen's Square, displays remains of part of the caldarium and hypocaust system excavated in 1930–31; this circulated hot air below the floor which was raised on pillars (*pilae*), warming up anyone relaxing in the caldarium. There are lots of descriptive displays illuminating all things Roman, and visitors (adults as well as children) are free to dress up in items from a superb collection of reproduction Roman clothing and military uniforms.

Blowing the cornu. A cornicen photographed during a re-enactment of Legio XV from Pram, Austria. The cornu was carried by the cornicen (horn-blower) who 'translated' his commander's orders into signals and broadcast them over the field during battles (courtesy of the Roman Bath Museum).

See:

Chrystal, Paul, *The Romans in the North of England*, Darlington, 2020.

Chrystal, Paul, *Roman York: A Historical Guide*, Barnsley, 2021.

Chrystal, Paul, *The Making of Roman York*, Lancaster, 2022.

48

All Saints, North Street

Your last 15 days on earth

A detail from the Doom Window showing the end of the world.

The first reference to a church here appears in 1089, but a church existed on the site before the Norman Conquest. The striking 120ft spire, erected in the late 14th century, is but one of this church's numerous treasures.

All Saints has some of the finest mediaeval stained glass in Europe that is not actually in York Minster, including the aisle window, which shows the Six Corporal Acts of Mercy (as in *Matthew*) and the famous 1410 Doom Window (or 'Pricke of Conscience' window), which graphically depicts *your* final 15 days on this earth before the Day of Judgement. The website says it best:

> *The first nine panels are concerned with the physical destruction of the earth. This begins with the seas rising and falling and giving up monsters that 'make a roaring that is hideous to man's hearing. Then follows the destruction of buildings by an earthquake (see the new-built spire of All Saints falling), and the burning of all physical matter. The last panels illustrate the fate of frightened mankind, and the end of all things. Men hide in holes, emerging only to pray. Finally on the fourteenth day 'all that lives then shall die, both children, men and women.' The end of things comes, the stars fall from the sky, the bones of the dead rise, and finally the 'the world burns on every side'.*
>
> - http://allsaints-northstreet.org.uk/stainedglass.html

The dramatic 1410 window is an apocalyptic vision of a world on fire, as in the last 15 days of the world before the Day of Judgement, and is as vivid a depiction of mediaeval terror and God-fearing repentance as you are likely to see anywhere. The captions are paraphrased (in English, not Latin) from the mediaeval poem *The Pricke of Conscience* – unusual for the time in view of low literacy levels amongst congregations and the prevalence of Latin in ecclesiastical settings. To some degree it is counter-balanced by the 'Corporal Acts of Mercy' window. The Acts of Mercy include feeding the hungry, offering drink to the thirsty, clothing the naked, visiting the sick and visiting those in prison, as in St Matthew's gospel.

Other marvels include a figure in one of the 14th-century windows wearing glasses – one of the earliest depictions of spectacles – and representations of the green man in the aisles and nave.

See:

Chrystal, Paul, *York's Churches & Places of Worship*, Catrine, 2016.

49

The Chapter House Ceiling

Ut Rosa flos florum, sic est Domus ista Domorum: *'As the Rose is Flower of Flowers, so this is the House of Houses'*

-Daniel Defoe, *A tour thro' the whole island of Great Britain*

If you were wowed by the Minster itself then prepare yourself for the splendour that is the Chapter House, contiguous to the main church. This octagonal building was completed in 1286 and was the official meeting place for the Dean and Chapter. The Chapter House is 63ft in diameter and about the same in height to the breathtaking ribbed vault of the dome; uniquely, it has no central pillar supporting the stunning domed roof and is one of the great masterpieces of mediaeval English carpentry. It was designed to emphasize the equality implicit in the Dean and Chapter: this explains the seven sets of six seats around the outside – not in the middle – and the intentionally poor acoustics, which meant that anyone speaking from the centre could barely be heard on the perimeter. Each seat is dedicated to a member of the Chapter. There are five magnificent stained-glass windows.

Canopied stalls around the walls below the windows have a fascinating set of over 250 carvings. The rich variety – some amusing, some terrifying, some shocking – represent aspects of the masons' own lives.

The beautiful ceiling.

> *It has been suggested that the set of figures represent simply an exuberance on the part of the original masons, and should be seen in the context of humorous additions tolerated by the commissioners of the structure, whimsical self-portraits, or expressions of independence of the craftsman over his temporal lords.*
>
> - Michael Tyler, *Symbols of Power and Authority: The Iconography of Late Thirteenth-Century Chapter Houses.*

Human heads, animals (monkeys, dogs and boars), puzzling allegorical figures, birds, plant foliage, and these with other carvings in the vestibule make up some of the finest mediaeval carvings in Europe, if not the world. One depicts a pair of lovers hiding behind one of the capitals.

See:

Chrystal, Paul, *York's Churches & Places of Worship*, Catrine, 2016.

50

Holy Trinity Church, Micklegate

Home to a marvellous mediaeval bestiary

In 1089 Benedictine monks from the Abbey of St Martin of Marmoutier near Tours, the 'Alien Benedictines', established a priory here on the site of a pre-Conquest church, itself possibly the successor of Alcuin of York's great Saxon church, the Alma Sophia. Why 'Aliens'? Because they were just that. The nave and tower are remnants of the Benedictine priory church, itself on the site of the pre-Conquest church that was known as Christ Church. It is listed in the *Domesday Book* as one of five great northern churches, along with York Minster, Durham, Beverley and Ripon, which were exempt from taxation. Holy Trinity-Christ Church was just as celebrated as the Minster in Saxon times; it was the first religious venue for travellers arriving in the city from the south and, later, where the Pilgrimage of Grace was fomented against Henry VIII's Reformation.

Richard II visited in 1397, and the tower collapsed in 1552. There are 18th-century stocks, which stood in the churchyard until 1858, and a memorial to Dr John Burton, historian and model for Dr Slop in Sterne's *Life & Times of Tristram Shandy, Gentleman*.

The feast of Corpus Christi seems to have received a boost in York in the early 15th century, following the 'martyrdom' of Archbishop Richard Scrope – executed for his role in a revolt against Henry IV in 1405 after Henry's 1399 victory over Richard III. Scrope was a Micklegate man: his family owned the church of St Martin in Micklegate, which was rebuilt, possibly incorporating a shrine to Scrope, some 20 years after his death. He was tried and executed in the fields of Clementhorpe near Holy Trinity – a chapel containing a reliquary of the saint's head was built nearby.

From the Holy Trinity Bestiary (MS61) reproduced by permission of the President and Fellows of St John's College, Oxford. These show the wolf and the bear. The wolf represented the Devil prowling round the sheepfold of the faithful. If the wolf trod on a branch near to the fold then it punished itself by biting the paw responsible. The female bear lived for three months underground after giving birth to formless lumps of flesh; she then licked them into the shape of cubs, from which we get our phrase 'licking into shape'.

Also from the Holy Trinity Bestiary (MS61), reproduced by permission of the President and Fellows of St John's College, Oxford. 'Adam Naming the Animals' – one of only six surviving bestiaries which includes an illustrated cycle of the Creation.

In 1413 a wooden cup, which Scrope had blessed, was bequeathed to the Corpus Christi fraternity in Holy Trinity Church. By the reign of Henry V, even the monarchy was venerating Scrope and sponsored the foundation of new religious houses in exculpation of their responsibility for his death. The so-called 'Bolton' Book of Hours, made about 1415 in York and connected with the Bolton family, is a product of this cult. It is sumptuously illuminated and focuses on a strong veneration for both Scrope and other northern and national saints. The significant image for us is one of Holy Trinity, around which the Bolton family is shown at prayer.

The 15th-century Jacob's Well form the parish rooms of Holy Trinity, Micklegate. The church now has an ongoing interactive exhibition for visitors on the monastic life of the priory entitled Monks of Micklegate. Extensive research included work at St John's College, Oxford, on a marvellous bestiary – an 800-page book of beasts with 90 beautifully coloured illustrations depicting Christian virtues as displayed by God's creation. This world-famous book was made by the monks of Holy Trinity. In 2010 'Micklegate Priory Revealed' was added to the 'Monks of Micklegate' exhibition:

> *An interactive touch screen that allows the visitor to experience the 15th-century Micklegate Priory, digitally reconstructed in a detailed 3D visualisation. Twelve areas of the priory can be investigated, including the cloister, the workshops, the gardens and the fishponds... Animations, accessible from within the reconstruction, present certain buildings and areas in more detail: visitors can see the dramatic tower collapse of 1550 and the devastating effect it had on the church, or take a virtual stroll around the gardens to see some of the plants that would have been grown and learn about their uses.*
>
> (www.holytrinityyork.org/monks)

See:

Chrystal, Paul, *York's Churches & Places of Worship,* Catrine, 2016.

51

Jacob's Well

The last vestiges of Clementhorpe Nunnery

The striking carved doorway.

Jacob's Well was built on the edge of the Priory precinct, in around 1474, with an endowment from Alderman Thomas Nelson. Alderman Nelson's gift enabled the building of a 'lodging chamber' for a chantry priest to pray three times a week for himself and his family in the Priory church. At the dissolution of the Priory next door in 1539, the house was bought by Dame Isabella Ward, the last Prioress of Clementhorpe Nunnery, for herself and her sister. Their brother was a brother in the Priory. In 1566, three years before her death, Ward made a Deed of Gift to the parishioners of Holy Trinity Church, to provide a Charity for the parish. The agreement was that she should be allowed to live in the house for the rest of her natural life on annual payment of a rent of one red rose, payable on Midsummer Day. On her death, the house would revert to the Trustees.

In around 1600 the house was converted into a two-storey building, and was originally a coach house, which later became an inn that consisted of a bar and a smoke room, and a taproom used as dining-room-cum-kitchen. Accommodation for the resident licensee was upstairs. The licence was eventually surrendered and transferred to a new public house in Nunnery Lane. In the early 1800s the innkeeper added a third storey in brick, thus over-loading the timber frame below. The church acquired the property in 1904 and the entrance in Trinity Lane was improved by the addition of carved entrance porch brackets and canopy, obtained from the Wheatsheaf Inn in Davygate, formerly the town house of the Bishop of Durham. York Butcher's Guild now use Jacob's Well as their Guild Hall.

52

The King's Arms: the Pub that's Never Dry

Or the pub that always floods

The pub in flood.

This is an early 17th-century building on King's Staith, traditionally a hotbed of crime and prostitution. Originally, the pub had no fireplaces or room partitions so it may have been a custom house, or a warehouse. Very thick walls protect it from floods, which recur to this day with alarming regularity. Due to the flooding, the cellars are on the first floor. Bodies of criminals were laid out here before being hung on and then flung from old Ouse Bridge just along the staith. It was first recorded as a pub in 1783 or 1795 as the King's Arms; then in the 19th century licensee George Duckitt renamed it as Ouse Bridge Inn. It reverted to its old name in 1974. The inn sign depicts King Richard III, who as a boy grew up at Middleham Castle, and as Duke of Gloucester visited York frequently from his castle at nearby Sheriff Hutton. Richard was very popular in York.

On the right-hand side of the door is a board with the flood levels marked on it. In 2000 the water was 6ft deep in the bar, deep enough to drown your sorrows in. Every time York floods – and that's a lot of times – the pub provides the backdrop for news reports broadcast the world over.

See:

Chrystal, Paul, *Pubs in and Around York*, Stroud, 2018.

53

The Troublesome Nuns of the Priory of St Clement

A nun's life: breakouts, 'lapses of the flesh', faking death

Detail from the Queen Mary Psalter showing three nuns with attitude. The Queen Mary Psalter (British Library, Royal MS 2 B.vii) is a 14th-century English psalter named after Mary I of England, who gained possession of it in 1553. The psalter is noted for its beauty and the lavishness of its illustration, and has been called 'one of the most extensively illustrated psalters ever produced in Western Europe' and 'one of the choicest treasures of the magnificent collection of illuminated MSS in the British Museum'.

Breakouts, 'lapses of the flesh' and faking death were just three of the indiscretions that the troublesome and truculent nuns of St Clement were guilty of. The Priory of St Clement, York, was founded by Thurstan of Bayeux, Archbishop of York, in or around 1130. This was the first monastic institution to be established in the north of England after the Norman Conquest. In 1189 Geoffrey (Geoffrey Plantagenet) was named Archbishop of York by his half-brother Richard I. Geoffrey was the acknowledged bastard son of Henry II. In 1192 he granted the priory of St Clement to the Abbey of Godstow, near Oxford, but the nuns were having none of it and appealed to the Pope; Alice the prioress journeyed personally to Rome to plead their case. The archbishop excommunicated the nuns, but with the papal decision in their favour they regained their independence.

Secular life was a problem for one of the nuns, a nun called Cecily. Late one evening in 1301 some men came to the priory gate leading a saddled horse. Cecily met them, and, throwing off her nun's habit, replaced it with a different robe and rode off with them to Darlington, where a certain Gregory de Thornton was waiting for her. She lived with him for the next three years or more.

Archbishop Greenfield dealt with the case of Joan de Saxton, another wayward nun, on whom a severe penance had been imposed for 'misbehaviour'. The archbishop mitigated the penance, but to avoid scandal Joan was confined to the cloister. For recreation and solace, she was allowed to go into the orchards and gardens of the monastery, accompanied by the other nuns. Twice a year she might receive friends in the presence of the prioress, or other nuns. In another stricture the archbishop further forbade the nuns to have girls over 12 years of age as boarders, and they were only permitted to keep washerwomen and other necessary servants in the house.

In 1317 Archbishop Melton ruled that secular women living in the house were not to converse with the nuns, lest evil suspicion should arise. Little girls, or males of any age whatever, or secular women, were not to be allowed to sleep in the dormitory with the nuns lest evil or scandal should transpire. Isabella de Stodley, a nun since 1315, had been found guilty of apostasy (a total desertion from one's religion), and *super lapsu carnis* (fornication), besides other transgressions. She was sent by Archbishop Melton to Yedingham near Malton to serve a penance in 1331.

Joan of Leeds did not enjoy being a nun. So she faked an illness, then faked her own death. Then to cap it all, she made a dummy in her likeness which was buried on holy ground. This is what Archbishop William Melton had to say about the ruse:

> *Out of a malicious mind simulating a bodily illness, she pretended to be dead, not dreading for the health of her soul, and with the help of numerous of her accomplices, evildoers, with malice aforethought, crafted a dummy in the likeness of her body… [she had] no shame in procuring its burial in a sacred space… She perverted her path of life arrogantly to the way of carnal lust and away from poverty and obedience. Having broken her vows and discarded the religious habit, she now wanders at large to the notorious peril to her soul and to the scandal of all of her order.*

Joan was discovered 30 miles away in Beverley, shacked up with a man. Archbishop Melton ordered her to return to the priory.

See:

Chrystal, Paul, *The Book: How the Wisdom of the Classical World Was Preserved – Writing, Publishing & Bookselling;* Barnsley, 2023.

Davenport, Cyril, *English embroidered bookbindings, The English bookman's library,* Vol. 1. London, 1899.

Facsimiles of Illuminated Manuscripts in Special Collections, 14th century: Queen Mary Psalter, University of Arizona, *2006.*

'Royal', McKendrick, Scott, Lowden, John and Doyle, Kathleen, (eds), *Royal Manuscripts, The Genius of Illumination*, 2011, British Library.

Stanton, Anne Rudloff. 'From Eve to Bathsheba and Beyond: Motherhood in the Queen Mary Psalter', in Taylor, Jane H. M. (ed.), *Women and the book: assessing the visual evidence. The British Library studies in medieval culture, Lesley Janette Smith,* Toronto, 1997.

Warner, George, *Queen Mary's Psalter Miniatures and Drawings by an English Artist of the 14th Century,* Reproduced from Royal Ms. 2 B. Vii in the British Museum (PDF)

54

Eccentric Frank Green and the Treasurer's House

'A bug-ridden slum'

Part of the superb interior. From www.realyorkshireblog.com/post/the-treasurers-house-york-frank-green-s-palace-of-entertainment, *Tim Barber, Real Yorkshire Tours.*

The Treasurer's House is a magnificent building in Minster Yard on the site of a building used by the Treasurer to the Minster until 1547. Radolphus was the first Treasurer in 1100; his special house was built on the site of the Roman garrison and was probably razed to the ground in the great fire of 1137. The present building combines a rebuild from around 1300 and a Grade 1-listed Jacobean town house with distinctive Flemish gables. Each room is laid out in the style of a different period, as instructed by Frank Green (1861–1954), who donated it, complete with contents, to the National Trust. The Parliamentarian General Sir Thomas Fairfax, of Marston Moor fame, once owned it, but by the 19th century it was reduced to a 'a bug ridden slum'. A Roman street, the Via Decumana, was excavated under the cellar in the 1960s, substantiating stories about ghostly legionaries.

The eccentric Green was educated at Eton and then Oxford, but he did not graduate. The young Frank had anger management issues from early days, once, for example, striking a tutor with a cricket bat. Whilst his brother's role was to raise the family's social position, Frank assisted his father in the management of the company that had factories in various countries.

The Greens moved to York in 1888 and lived at Nunthorpe Hall, overlooking York racecourse, to satisfy their passion for horse racing and hunting. Frank bought three-fifths of a York property next to York Minster in 1897–98 and commissioned architect Temple Lushington Moore to oversee extensive alterations and restoration. Frank called the result 'Treasurer's House' and it became a show-case for his impressive collection of *objets d'art* and antique furniture.

He and the Green family were active

philanthropists in Wakefield, Norfolk and York, supporting many causes and public works, including York Minster. Frank passed his time travelling around Europe in one of his several Rolls-Royce cars for leisure and for purchasing items for his collection.

Green was an enthusiastic entertainer, especially enjoying the company of actors and musicians including Ellen Terry. In York he frequently organised lavish society balls, for example the York Bachelors' Ball. His footmen would be dressed as bewigged page boys to serve guests from gold plates. He was himself a fastidious dresser, changing his clothes at least three times a day. His trademark outfit was a bowler hat and a hand-tied bow tie, but he also enjoyed frilled shirts and capes. While abroad he often purchased items of national costume.

Frank Green's bad temper accompanied him throughout his life and he clearly exhibited signs of obsessive compulsive disorder: his obsessions with cleanliness and hygiene had to be obeyed to the letter. Staff were required to meet exacting standards following personal inspections of the kitchens and other rooms. He was known to visit the kitchens late at night, just to check that cutlery was stored correctly. Chunks of coal had to be wrapped individually before they were put in the fireplace. His laundry was sent by train to London for service. Once, when a fly was spotted in the kitchen, Frank ordered all food in the house to be immediately destroyed. He is, however, most famous for the metal studs he had placed in the floor of Treasurer's House to indicate precisely where a table or chair leg had to be. He later threatened to come back and haunt Treasurer's House if any items of his collection were moved.

See:

'The Treasurer's House and Gray's Court', *An Inventory of the Historical Monuments in City of York, Volume 5, Central,* London, 1981, pp. 69–76.

History of York: Treasurer's House, York Museums Trust.

55

Rowntree Park Reading Café

Coffee, cakes, books – perfection

The Reading café

Located in the lovely setting that is Rowntree Park on the River Ouse, this innovative, unusual cafe is a vibrant family-friendly space serving breakfast and home-cooked food daily. The menu is seasonal, with fresh, locally sourced ingredients used wherever possible.

Rowntree Park café is part of the city's 'York Explore Library and Archive' and offers a full library service including lots of books to borrow or browse.

There are other reading cafés at Tang Hall (Burnholme) and at Hungate in Bellerby Ct.

56

The Inner Space Station, Hull Road

Your last stop before Mars

Some of the security at https://innerspacestations.com/

Forget about the boring old petrol pumps, the container storage area and the self-storage facilities, the run-of-the-mill petrol station shop and the car wash, this 1990s petrol station is the last stop before Mars, staffed by intergalactic heroes ensuring that security is out of this world.

57

County Industries Ltd

Rowntree munitions workers, 1943.

As with other companies, normal output and service was suspended at Rowntrees during World War II to aid the war effort. For example, Cadbury (masquerading as Bournville Utilities Ltd) turned out aircraft seats and part of the Bournville factory was let to Austin to produce aircraft gun magazines and helmets, and to Lucas to increase rotating gun turret and sten gun magazine production. The Moulding Department produced gun doors for Spitfires, air-intake and super-charger controls for Stirlings while Metals turned out pilots' seats for Defiants, junction boxes for Wellingtons and upper-mid gun turrets for Stirlings; other departments churned out jerry cans, fuel tanks for Spitfires, Beaufighters, Lancasters and Vosper motor torpedo boats.

A prodigious amount of impromptu management and reorganisation went into converting Haxby Road into what was virtually a munitions factory. Much of this presumably fell to Seebohm and Arnold Rowntree.

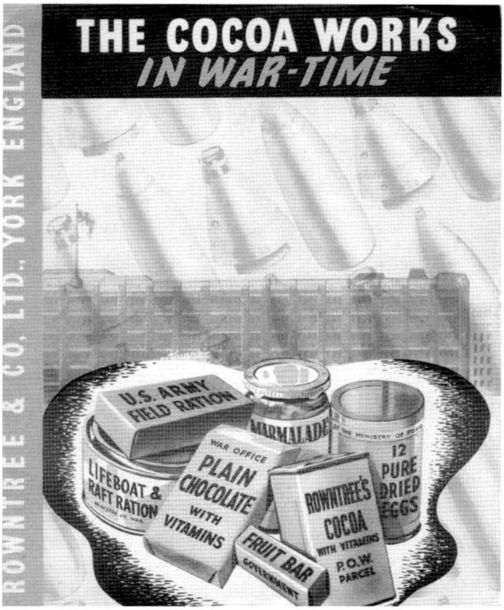

Rowntree CWM war special.

The definitive record of this fascinating chapter in the wartime lives of the staff, board and management at Rowntrees can be found in *The Cocoa Works in War-time* published by the company soon after the end of hostilities; here are some of the details recorded there: 13,000 square feet of floor space in the new office block was put at the disposal of 300 clerks of the Royal Army Pay Corps. The Fruit Gum Department, at the request of the Ministry Of Food, manufactured jams and marmalade for Frank Cooper Ltd of Oxford. Part of the Almond Block extension was used by York firm Cooke, Troughton & Simms for the manufacture of military optical instruments. From the Cream Department came ersatz products such as *National Milk Cocoa, Ryvita, Household Milk* and *Dried Egg.*

The site next to the sports ground was chosen for the storage of explosives for County Industries Ltd (CIL), a company set up mainly to produce shell and mine fuses and housed in the Smarties block. The Card Box Mill replaced its production of fancy boxes to become a main supply depot for the R.A.S.C. Northern Command. The rest centre in the Dining Block was a refuge for blitzed families mainly in the aftermath of the Baedeker raid after which it was requisitioned for five nights; a VAD hospital with 100 or so beds occupied the rest of the building. The nursery was also in there; this allowed mothers of children aged six months to five years of age to come to work. At any one time sixty children were looked after; cots and other furniture was made by the work's joiners and the orchard behind the Dining Block became the playground.

The target for CIL set by the Ministry of Supply was 100,000 fuses per week, made mainly for shells used in twenty-five pounder guns; this was exceeded. By the end of the war CIL had also turned out four million anti-tank mine fuses. Workers in contact with explosive powder had to protect their skin and so 'make up' rooms were set up where special face powder and topical creams were made available. Girls and women were advised to drink milk rather than tea or coffee at their mid-shift break. The sixty men and 850 women here worked alternate day and night shifts and were under the management of the aptly named Mr N.G. Sparkes; most of them had been transferred from production work in the Cocoa Works.

ARP work included the construction of three underground tunnel shelters in the orchard, rose garden and near the Wigginton Road entrance. The fire brigade comprised twenty-three full time and eighty part time staff, complemented by 145 fire guards. The air raid siren was on the top of the Elect Cocoa Block – throughout the war it sounded 140 times in blasts that lasted for 209 hours in total. The Estates Department was busy digging for victory: between 1939 and 1945 eight tons each of tomatoes, cabbage and onions, three tons of leeks and two tons of Brussels sprouts and 13,000 heads of lettuce along with smaller quantities of other vegetables were produced.

One of the most productive departments in the factory was the Cake (Chocolate Moulding) Department which was engaged in the production of various types of war-time chocolate. Vitaminised plain chocolate was made for army rations and for distribution by U.N.R.R.A. for the relief of starving children in Europe. Blended chocolate and vitaminised Plain York Chocolate was made for prisoner-of-war parcels; at Christmas these were sent out with special wrappers.

Special chocolate 'Naps' in sealed tins were supplied to the Ministry of War Transport as emergency rations for use on ships, lifeboats and rafts. Pacific and Jungle chocolate was specially produced to withstand high temperatures for troops and sailors in tropical climates. A similar type of 'unmeltable' chocolate is still produced in Australian chocolate factories today. Oatmeal Block and Fruit Bar was made for the servicemen in the Far East. U.S. Army Field Ration Vitaminised chocolate, known as ration D, was specially packed for the American forces. An Army Emergency Ration Special Chocolate that was hermetically sealed in tins was also manufactured along with special chocolate rations for use by air crew after baling out.

See:

Chrystal, Paul, *A History of Chocolate in York,* Barnsley, 2012.

Rothnie, Niall, *The Baedeker Blitz.* Ian Allan, 1992.

Kessler, Leo, Taylor, Eric, *The York Blitz, 1942: The Baedeker Raid on York,* York, 1986.

58

York Cold War Bunker, Holgate

The place to go just before the bomb drops

The bunker today.

York's worst kept secret opened, or rather closed, in 1961. This piece of Cold War furniture was officially No 20 Group Royal Observer HQ operated by UKWMO, the UK Warning and Monitoring Organisation. Its role was to function as one of the UK's 29 monitoring and listening posts in the event of a nuclear explosion; the bunker was designed as a nerve-centre to monitor fallout and explosions in the event of a nuclear attack on York.

The building would have supported 60 local volunteer members of the Royal Observer Corps, including a ten-man United Kingdom Warning and Monitoring Organisation scientific warning team. The 60 people, working round the clock in three watches, would have lived in the Holgate bunker for about a month after a nuclear attack. They had a 30-day supply of food, mainly dehydrated military rations.

York is the only bunker that is preserved in its operational condition. The others are derelict or have either been demolished or sold. A few have been repurposed, like No. 16 Group Shrewsbury, which is now a veterinary clinic, another is a recording studio, two are satellite and communications control centres, and one is a solicitor's file storage facility.

Decommissioned in 1991, English Heritage have, after a £240,000 restoration, opened York's fascinating two-storey, semi-subterranean building to the public to enable them to see the decontamination areas, living quarters, communications centre and operations rooms. Visitors will also see air filtration and generating plant, kitchen and canteen, dormitories, radio and landline communication equipment and specialist 1980s computers and a fully equipped operations room with vertical illuminated perspex maps.

The bunker offers a truly unique experience as it's unlikely that any of us would have enjoyed the relative security it offered to a chosen few.

See:

'Cold War bunker, Holgate, York', *The Press, 4 August 2007.*

Historic England, *No 20 Group Royal Observer Corps Headquarters (1310348), Research records (formerly PastScape).*

59

Houses of Correction

Bone crushing and 'a terror to evil-doers'

Police Station with cell in Kirkgate, York Castle Museum.

These were establishments built after the passing of the Elizabethan Poor Law (1601), places where those who were 'unwilling to work', including vagrants, were 'persuaded' to work.

Due to the first reformation of manners campaign, the late 17th century was marked by the growth in the number of houses of correction, often generically termed *bridewells*, established by the passage of numerous statutes prescribing them as the punishment for specific minor offences. The Society for the Reformation of Manners was founded in the Tower Hamlets area of London in 1691. Its aims were the suppression of profanity, immorality, and other lewd activities in general, and of brothels and prostitution in particular. The society flourished until the 1730s.

In the Middlesex and Westminster houses of correction in the late-17th and early 18th centuries the most common charges against prisoners were prostitution, petty theft, and 'loose, idle and disorderly conduct' (a loosely defined offence which could involve a wide range of misbehaviour). Over two-thirds of the prisoners were women.

More than half of offenders were released within a week, and two-thirds within two weeks. In addition to imprisonment in a house of correction, over half of the convicted were whipped, particularly those found guilty of theft, vagrancy, and lewd conduct and nightwalking (prostitution).

Virtually all the prisoners were required to do hard labour, typically beating hemp.

In 1720 an act allowed the use of houses of corrections for pre-trial detention of 'vagrants, and other criminals, offenders, and persons charged with minor offences'. By the 1760s and 1770s, prisoners awaiting trial accounted for more than three-quarters of those committed to the Middlesex and Westminster houses.

There were two houses of correction in York: one on Old Baile from 1807, the other on Toft Green from 1814. The provision of a tread-wheel seems to have exercised the authorities for some time before one was installed in 1825 – 'a terror to evil-doers'. A typical wheel would have been 5ft in diameter with 24 steps holding 24 convicts taking 45 steps per minute for ten hours in the summer and seven in winter. The (often disregarded) maximum was limited to 12,000ft in ascent in one day or just under three miles.

Many simply 'ground air', but at Toft Green the authorities found a commercial angle when they used it in an adjacent bone house (animal bone that is) for bone crushing. Unfortunately the wheel here was also used as a ladder of escape, which led to its removal from the wall. It was taken away completely in 1833 and prisoners reverted to smashing boulders.

See:

'The 1601 Elizabethan Poor Law', www.victorianweb.org.

'Background – Houses of Correction – London Lives', www.londonlives.org.

'The New Billerica House of Correction'.

Innes, J, 'Prisons for the Poor: English Bridewells, 1555-1800', in Snyder, F. and Hay, D. eds, *Labour, Law and Crime: An Historical Perspective,* 1987, pp. 42-122.

Shoemaker, Robert B, *Prosecution and Punishment: Petty Crime and the Law in London and Rural Middlesex*, Cambridge, 1991.

60

The Mansion House and the Dead Cat

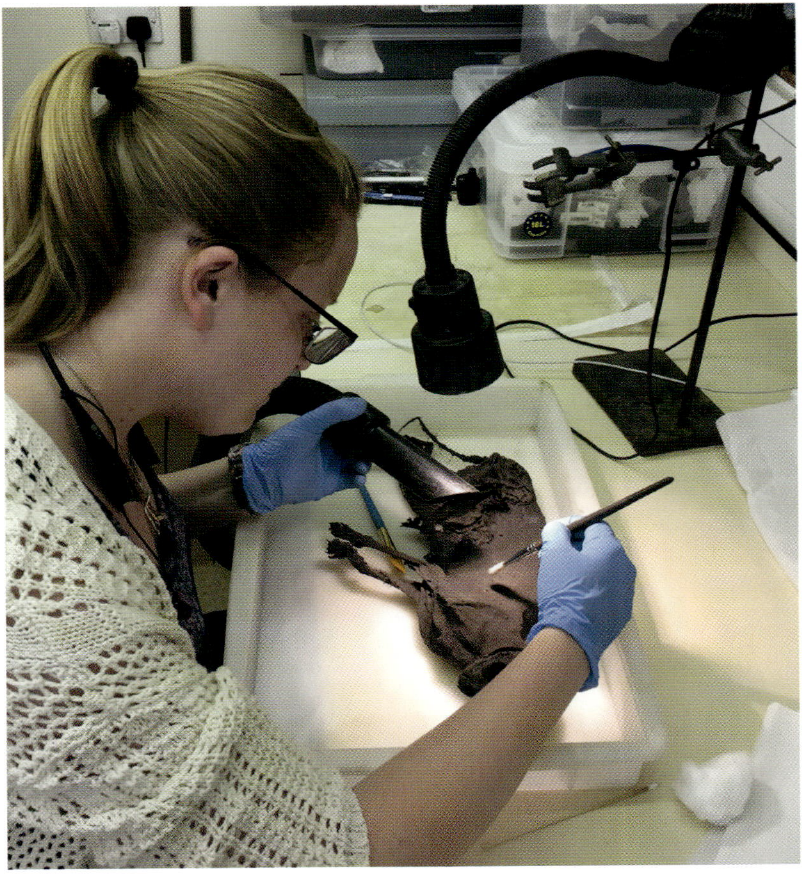

YAT's Chelsea Blake working on the mummified cat (with permission of York Archaeological Trust).

Shades of Edgar Allen Poe's horror story *'The Black Cat'* (1843) can be sensed in the 'Cabinet of Curiosities' in the Mansion House. On 20 August 2020 *York Archaeology* reported on a bizarre find during their dig during an extensive restoration. 'The Curious Case of the Mansion House Cat' reports that:

> *One of the most surprising finds was a mummified cat, located in the state room ceiling, between the plaster and laths. The cat was either placed in the house in 1732 when the ceiling was built or in 1830 when the upper floors became more domestic. Interestingly the cat was surrounded by hazelnut shells.*

Enter YAT Conservator Chelsea Blake, who commented that, 'It was common at the time for cats to be buried in walls or under floors as an apotropaic symbol (apotropaic means supposedly having the power to avert evil influences or bad luck).'

With that cleared up, Chelsea adds: 'The conservation process involved analysing samples of the insect remains and the hair still intact, before a freeze-drying process so no mould spores or insect activity could return. There's so much history preserved in the body of the cat.'

X-Rays by Tower Vet Groups in York established that the cat was between one and two years old, and dead when it was put under the floorboards. It was placed in such a way as to make it look like it was sleeping.

The cat is now on display in the 'Cabinet of Curiosities' in Mansion House.

61

Pavement

Woman for sale: 7s 6d, including halter

Pavement about 1900, Courtesy of York Press.

Pavement is called thus because in around 1329 it was the only clear piece of paved land in the centre of the city. Paving was unusual then. Before that it was called Marketshire and was the site of markets (there once was a fine market cross here), proclamations and public punishments in days when the punishment was made, and seen, to fit the crime: for example, drunks were made to stand on barrels with pint pots on their heads and goose thieves were put in the stocks with goose wings draped unceremoniously around their necks. Catholic Thomas Percy, Earl of Northumberland, was executed here in 1572 for his opposition to Elizabeth I. The wonderful Market Cross was demolished in 1813 to make room for more market stalls.

But for a York street named so underwhelmingly, this thoroughfare has enjoyed a most colourful history. Here are some of its highlights:

A veritable menagerie and a constant hive of activity; all life was here. *Ye Old Streete of Pavement,* written by W Camidge in 1893 and published by the *Yorkshire Gazette,* provides a colourful, vivid picture of activity there over the years. We read of the Goose Flags – the path in front of St Crux signifying the goose market there; boots and shoes on sale 'in Whip-ma-whop-ma-gate, where members of the "Worshipful Company of Translators" sold these commodities, old and new' and 'the basket market… at the bottom of Colliergate'. The pleasure fairs 'at Whitsuntide and Martinmas', and the shows that accompanied them, were very popular too: there were dog and lion fights 'and other shows with fat women, deformed men, giants and dwarfs, reptiles, waxworks, mechanical inventions, fortune tellers, circuses, boxing booths', along with swing boats and hobby horses. Peep shows were particularly popular:

> *Their incidents stirring, and their pictures very striking… chiefly battles… Waterloo and the crossing of the Alps by Napoleon… described by the showman in measured and monotonous tones in which fact and fancy were mixed up in most bewildering confusion.*

On most Saturdays there were auction sales in Pavement:

> *Not the least interesting was the sale of a woman [in 1839]. She had left her husband through his drunken habits and ill-treatment, and in one of his mad freaks he had brought her into the Market-place… with a halter round her neck. She was mounted on a table beside the auctioneer, who descanted on her virtues and spoke of her as a clean, industrious, quiet and careful woman, attractive in appearance and well mannered.*

She went for 7s 6d, halter included, and proceeded to live with her purchaser near to Pavement. Twenty years later her husband died and she married said purchaser; she herself died in the 1880s 'at a great age, respectable and respected'.

Camidge gives a graphic account of the near anarchy and corruption which attended local elections:

> *It was not unusual during the progress of an election to roll into the Pavement large barrels of ale, one end of which was speedily knocked in, and then a scene of indescribable confusion and contention ensued. Men, women and children rushed for the beer barrel, and with every description of kitchen and other utensils they sought to drink their fill,*

> *and carry off what unsteady legs, and intense excitement would allow them to get away with. It was no uncommon thing as the beer neared the bottom for someone to fall, or be pushed into the barrel.*

Pavement and Minster Yard were *'proverbial for fights'* – the latter because of the ready supply of staves as:

> *The Minster was at that time encircled with wood palisades… one man… dyed his whiskers and hair to the colour he had voted, but found himself minus much of his hair before he escaped from the crowd.*

Camidge tells us that 'public-houses were also opened as "free houses" where an elector on producing a ticket could have a free drink'; this cost one candidate in 1830 around £1,200.

Before the completion of the tunnel, a number of firms sold concertina paper peepshows that gave a three-dimensional view of what the tunnel would look like when completed. As the world's first tunnel under a river, it was a marvel of engineering and attracted a lot of attention during its construction, and these paper cut-out models were very popular.

When the Thames Tunnel opened in 1843 it was actually a bit of a flop, as there wasn't enough money to build the huge ramps to get road vehicles down to the tunnel. So, it opened as a pedestrian only tunnel.

See:

Camidge, W, *Ye Old Streete of Pavemente, Yorkshire Gazette,* York, 1893.

62

The King David Panel

A treasure in Fairfax House

Artworks go missing all the time, especially, it seems, masterpieces. The King David Panel by Grinling Gibbons (1648–1721) is one such treasure, which disappeared for 300 years or so but is now safely and impressively installed in York's Fairfax House. The Anglo-Dutch sculptor and wood carver can count in his portfolio splendid work at Windsor Castle, Petworth House (the Carved Room), St Paul's Cathedral and Hampton Court Palace, and now at York's Fairfax House.

Born in Rotterdam, after training Gibbons arrived in England aged 19 looking for day-to-day work as a decorative carver in York and later in Deptford – the centre of British naval shipbuilding. Patronage by celebrities, such as the author John Evelyn and artist Peter Lely, led to royal patronage under Charles II, first at Windsor Castle and later, in 1693, as the King's Master Carver.

His time in York produced the small but mightily impressive King David Panel around 1670. The piece measures 37cm x 24cm and is carved in high relief sculpture, meaning it is carved deeply from the background. Made from boxwood, the panel was seamed together from two pieces of wood. The subject is copied from Peter Candid's *c.* 1589–93 painting *The Performance of a Motet of Orlando di Lasso,* which Gibbons would have known via Johannes Sadeler's (1550–1600) engraving of the work. It depicts King David playing a harp and singing, surrounded by other instrumentalists and dancing cherubs. The scene is a reference to the biblical Psalm 148, 'Praise the Lord'. About 100 years later the image from the engraving was painted on glass for two prominent families in York, the Barwicks and the Fairfaxes.

The King David Panel presumably spent most of its lost 300 years in private collections, emerging back on the art scene in a 1963 auction at Sothebys in London.

From there, it was in the private collection of Cyril Humphries, a London art dealer, who sold his collection in 1995, via Sothebys, which had by that time moved to New York. The next known owner was A Alfred Taubman, another private collector, and coincidentally the owner of Sotheby's NY. Mr Taubman passed away in 2015 and his private collection was sold in 2016. The King David panel was purchased by the art collectors, Tomasso Brothers, and brought back to Leeds… It appeared in 2016, once again available for sale, and in danger of being sold again to someone abroad.
www.grinlinggibbonsphotos.com/fairfax-house/

To avoid what would have been a tragic loss, Fairfax House set in train a determined fundraising campaign, and by 17 October the panel was in York's Fairfax House where it is on display.

The Fairfax House website tells us that:

The painting and print is based on Psalms 148 and 150, and depict a visionary concert led by King David, playing a harp and ringed by dancing cherubs. Above David, in the heavenly realms, angelic musicians are accompanied by St Cecilia, the patron saint of music. The panel features an array of musical instruments from an organ to a viola di gamba as well of course as David's own harp. The music being played, held up for viewers to see by flying cherubs, is a motet by Orlando di Lasso.

Fairfax House

Born in 1723, John Carr was Lord Mayor of York in 1770 and 1785. He lived on his estate at Askham Richard for most of his adult life. He designed the Crescent at Buxton; racecourse grandstands at York, Doncaster and Nottingham, prisons at Wakefield and Northallerton, Greta Bridge, Constable Burton Hall and Harewood House. His crowning achievement though is the magnificent Fairfax House in Castlegate, York.

One of the finest Georgian town houses in England, Fairfax House was originally the winter home of Viscount Fairfax, having been purchased in 1760 as a dowry to Anne Fairfax. Its richly decorated interior was redesigned in the classical style by York architect John Carr, with its magnificent staircase, ceilings, Venetian window and iron balusters. Adapted in the last century for use as a cinema and dance hall (St George's), Fairfax House was restored to its former glory by York Civic Trust in 1982–84. Sir Simon Jenkins said of it in 2003 'it is the most perfect 18th century townhouse I have come across anywhere

The King David panel.

in England.' The Noel Terry collection of furniture, clocks, paintings and decorative arts, described by Christie's as one of the finest private collections of the 20th century, furnish and embellish the house.

See:

Beard, Geoffrey, *The Work of Grinling Gibbons*, John Murray, 1989.

Esterly, David, *Grinling Gibbons and the Art of Carving*, V&A Publications, 2000.

Webb, Gerry (2001), *Fairfax of York: The Life & History of a Noble Family*, York

63

Elizabeth Montague

'Queen of the Blues'

'Breaking Up of the Blue-stocking Club' 1815, hand-coloured etching on paper by Thomas Rowlandson (1756–1827).

Grays Court is the oldest continuously occupied house in the country – parts of it date back to 1080 when it was commissioned by the first Norman Archbishop of York, Thomas de Bayeux. It was the original Treasurer's House.

Grays Court exudes history: James I dined here with Edmund, Lord Sheffield, the Lord President of the North, knighting eight noblemen in the Long Gallery in one evening. Sir Thomas Fairfax owned Grays Court between 1649 and 1663, during which time he laid siege to the

city. James Duke of York and Maria Beatrix of Modena, his wife, later King and Queen, stayed in Grays Court in 1679.

Elizabeth Montague was born here in 1718. She founded the Blue-stocking Club 'where literary topics were to be discussed, but politics, gossip and card-playing were barred'. *Elizabeth Montagu* (née Robinson; 1718–1800) was a British social reformer, patron of the arts, *salonnière*, literary critic and writer. She devoted the family fortune to developing English and Scottish literature and to the relief of the poor.

The Encyclopaedia Britannica defines 'blue-stocking' as 'any of a group of women who in mid-18th-century England held "conversations" to which they invited men of letters and members of the aristocracy with literary interests'. The word has come to be applied pejoratively to a woman who affects literary or learned interests and was, is, synonymous with 'frumpy' or 'fishwife'. Romantic William Hazlitt said, 'The blue-stocking is the most odious character in society… she sinks where she is placed, like the yolk of an egg, to the bottom, and carries the filth with her.' Other male detractors such as Lord Byron and Samuel Coleridge also derided the blue-stockings.

Lydia Figes tells us the group was:

Often defined as radical for being the first female-led group to champion the careers of other women, in many ways the group was, in fact, rather conservative in its initial aims.

The blue-stockings defined themselves by what they were not, *standing against the debauched hedonism of 18th-century high society that encouraged excessive drinking, gambling, and idle tittle-tattle. They regarded themselves as virtuous proponents for the art of refined and intellectual conversation, usually over tea drinking.*

The name derives from 'the informal blue worsted stockings worn by members of the circle, who preferred this attire over the formal silk black stockings'. Protocol demanded that women and men separated after social meals, but the blue-stockings encouraged guests to remain together to engage in intellectual conversation.

Portrait of Elizabeth Montagu

Figes adds:

Significantly, Montagu was the richest woman in England, who was born into gentry but married into aristocracy when she was betrothed to Edward Montagu. A formidable character and celebrity in 18th-century society, she was named 'Queen of the blues' and was regarded as the leading lady of the blue-stockings, harnessing the power of her social connections and witty repartee.

See:

Eger, Elizabeth (2008). Brilliant women: 18th-century bluestockings, New Haven, CT.

Figes, Lydia, https://artuk.org/discover/stories/who-were-the-bluestockings#tells.

Hill, Bridget (2010). 'A Tale of Two Sisters: The Contrasting Careers And Ambitions of Elizabeth Montagu And Sarah Scott', *Women's History Review*, 19 (2): 215–229.

Myers, Sylvia Harcstark, *The Bluestocking Circle: Women, Friendship, and the Life of the Mind in Eighteenth-Century England*, Oxford, 1990.

Pohl, Nicole Reconsidering the Bluestockings, San Marino, Calif: Huntington Library, 2003, pp. 30–31, 60, 105, 263.

Pohl, Nicole, The Commerce of Life': Elizabeth Montagu (1718–1800), Huntington Library Quarterly, 81 (4): 443–463.

64

Mary Ellen Best

Kitchen sink social history artist

'The Artist at Work', Mary Ellen Best (1809-1891) (York Art Gallery, YORAG: R2396, York Museums Trust).

Mary Ellen Best (1809–1891) produced most of her work in the 1830s, usually working in watercolour, often painting scenes of domestic life. She was born in York in 1809, the daughter of doctor Charles Best of Bootham Park Hospital from 1804–1815, and his wife, Mary Norcliffe Dalton. Best grew up on Little Blake Street near York Minster.

She depicted families at tables, kitchens and domestic staff. She painted a number of water-colours of her home in Castlegate, including interior portraits of the drawing room, dining room (1838), and one of herself working in her painting room. She also painted other houses including the drawing room of Naburn Hall, which was then home to George Palmes. After marrying Johan Anton and moving to Nuremberg, Frankfurt, Worms, and Darmstadt, she continued to paint the houses they lived in.

Between 1828 and 1840, two-thirds of Best's portraits were commissioned by women. Caroline Davidson, Best's biographer, calculated that she produced more than 1,500 paintings in total.

Some of Best's drawings were handed down to her great-granddaughter, and forty-seven were sold in January 1983 in New York City, though York Art Gallery obtained three of them. The paintings are of historical interest as a record of Yorkshire and European life in the 1830s and 1840s.

'The Sideboard', Mary Ellen Best (1809-1891) (York Art Gallery, YORAG: R2400, York Museums Trust).'The Sideboard', Mary Ellen Best (1809-1891) (York Art Gallery, YORAG: R2400, York Museums Trust).

See:

Balducci, Temma, *Negotiating Identity: Mary Ellen Best and The Status of Female Victorian Artists,* Nineteenth-Century Art Worldwide, 2015.

Brockbank, Jonathan, *York: A Virtual Cultural/Historical Tour: York in the late 18th early 19th Century: Female Creativity, Leisure and Class,* Department of English, University of York.

Cornforth, John, 'An anticipation of Victoriana. The drawings of Mary Ellen Best', *Country Life,* pp. 1549–1552, 9 June 1983.

Davidson, Caroline, *The World of Mary Ellen Best, London, 1985.*

Digby, Anne, *From York Lunatic Asylum to Bootham Park Hospital (Issue 69 Borthwick Papers), York: St. Anthony's Press, 1986.*

65

The City Walls Experience

'Off with his head and set it on York's gates; so York did overlook the town of York –
Shakespeare, Queen Margaret in Henry VI

A scene from the City Walls Experience, brought to you by the people who created the Jorvik Viking Experience.

Opened in 2022, this fascinating museum can be found on two floors in Micklegate Bar on York's splendid city walls. Inside, the visitor will discover 'pageantry and barbaric history which has unfolded between these historic walls over several centuries'. The museum is the work of the people who brought the Jorvik Viking Centre to York.

The Hello Yorkshire website (www.hello-yorkshire.co.uk/micklegate-bar-museum-york) tells how the Bar itself is a 'gateway to the city from the south and also a home to many families until 1918, not just the living people occupied Micklegate Bar. Heads of traitors and tyrants from across York's history were displayed here after execution for all of York's population to bear witness to.'

Micklegate Bar was originally called Mickleith, which means great gate; the royal arms are those of Edward III; the arch is Norman, the rest 14th century, and the side arch was added in 1753.

Being on the road to and from London, this was the Bar through which royal visitors entered York. Edward IV, Richard III, Henry VII, Margaret Tudor, James I, Charles I (on three Civil War occasions) and James II all passed through. Henry VIII was scheduled to enter here but, in the event, came in through Walmgate Bar. Heads and quarters of traitors were routinely displayed on the top – most famously, Lord Scrope of Mastan in 1415; Sir Henry Percy (Hotspur) after his part in the rebellion against Elizabeth I; Richard Duke of York after the Battle of Wakefield in 1460, prompting Shakespeare to write, 'Off with his head and set it on York's gates; so York did overlook the town of York' (Queen Margaret in *Henry VI);* and Thomas Percy in 1569 – whose head remained there for two years. Removal of heads without permission was, appropriately, punishable by beheading – guess where the heads ended up? The last displays were in 1746 after the Jacobite Rebellion at Culloden. The heads of James Mayne and William Connelly remained on the Bar until 1754. The barbican was removed in 1826 to allow a circus access to the city; the east side arch was built in 1827.

In November 2022, King Charles III made his first formal visit to York as monarch, entering through Micklegate Bar. The King and his wife, the Queen Consort, Camilla, came to York to unveil a statue of the late Queen at York Minster. In a break with tradition, in April 2023 Charles and Camilla did not enter through the Bar when they arrived for their Maundy visit.

It was in April 2012, that the late Queen Elizabeth II entered the city via Micklegate Bar.

66

Barley Hall

'A warren of tradesmen's workshops'

Barley Hall, Christmas 2022 (courtesy of York Press).

Parts of Barley Hall go back as far as 1360, when the Hall was built as the York town house for Nostell Priory, the Augustinian monastery near Wakefield, by Thomas de Dereford, the Prior from 1337 to 1372. The Priors of Nostell were prebendary canons of York Minster and attended ceremonies, services and business meetings in the city; a hostel, therefore, made good commercial sense. However, by the 15th century, the Priory had fallen on hard times and Barley Hall was leased out to private tenants. A new wing was added in about 1430, and in 1460 it was rented out to William Snawsell – goldsmith, Master of the Royal Mint in York, MP for York, Alderman and Lord Mayor of York in 1468. By the 17th century it was subdivided into a number of smaller dwellings so that the 'screens passage' – the internal corridor area at the end of the Great Hall – came to be used as a public short-cut through from Stonegate to Swinegate. To this day it remains a public right-of-way, known as Coffee Yard. By Victorian times, the house was 'a warren of tradesmen's workshops' and its last use before being sold for redevelopment in 1984 was as a plumber's workshop and showroom. The hall was painstakingly restored to its former glory as it would have been in 1483, and it re-opened to the public in 1993. Barley Hall is named after Professor Maurice Barley, founder president of York Archaeological Trust.

Barley Hall

See:

Gerrard, p.214; *Barley Hall, Coffee Yard, York: Reconstruction of 14th century monastic hospice,* Archived 14 March 2011 at the Wayback Machine, McCurdy and Co. Ltd.

67

Meet Eymund at the Jorvik Viking Centre

'You are standing on the site of one of the most famous and astounding discoveries of modern archaeology'

Animatronic tableau of fishermen working and talking at the Jorvik Viking Centre, York (photographer: Chemical Engineer).

Meet Eymund. He was a Viking fisherman and very much a part of daily life in Viking York as delineated in the AD 975 Jorvik Cityscape there. Eymund is a disturbingly faithful reconstruction from a Viking skeleton excavated in Fishergate in York. In 1990, when cutting-edge computer technology allowed for the first time the affordable reconstruction of faces from the past, York Archaeological

Trust used a skeleton from 10th-century burials at Fishergate to literally bring visitors face to face with the Vikings and their world. The result was a highly realistic presence gazing out at you from the 1,000-year-plus past. Eymund is joined by Thorfast, the antler bone carver; Lothin, the wood turner; Snarri, the jeweller; and Svein, the leather worker – all toiling away in their workshops and stalls. Other exhibits feature the toilets, wells, warehouses, workshops and homes faithfully reproduced from the major discoveries by archaeologists from the York Archaeological Trust. The result is a fascinating, almost living, picture of Viking life in 10th-century Jorvik, with noises, smells and sights evoking another world, all conveyed in Time Cars, which silently glide you back through the years.

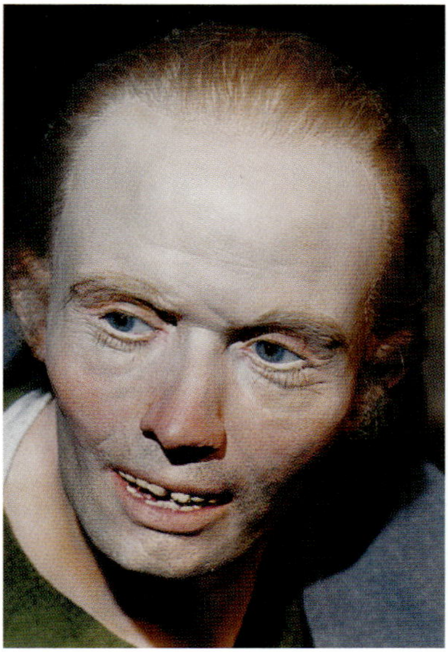

Eymund

Beyond this is an extensive museum area, which combines an exhibition of some 800 finds from the site with interactive displays and the opportunity to learn about 10th-century life and to discuss it with 'Viking' staff. Among the exhibits is a replica of the famous Coppergate Helmet, which was found near the site of the centre and is now in the Yorkshire Museum.

68

Snickelways

Lose yourself in the essence of mediaeval York

Gaslit snickelway; from https://www.awaywithmaja.com/best-snickelways-in-york/ *Lady Peckett's Yard with JH Storey, cordwainer, at the end.*

Snickelways are back alleys – a network of narrow pedestrian-only alleyways which spider their way across the city. The word is a neologism coined by Mark Jones in his 1983 *A Walk Around the Snickelways of York*; it is a compound of *snicket*, a walled passageway; *ginnel*, a narrow passageway between buildings, and *alleyway*, a narrow street or lane. In York, examples include Mad Alice Lane, Hornpot Lane, Mucky Peg Lane, Hole in the Wall, Pope's Head Alley, and Coffee Yard (Langton Lane). *The Snickleway* (sic) Inn in Goodramgate was originally called *The Anglers* because it was close to the Minster stonemasons' yard – an angler being a geometrist working on the stones. This follows a long tradition of being named after artisans: previous names also include *The Painters' Arms, The Square & Compass* and *The Board.*

See:

Jones, Mark W, *A Walk Around the Snickelways of York,* York, 2010.

Some examples:

Little Peculiar Lane, off Petergate, is the shortest of all York's snickelways and probably the most appealing due to its breathtaking views of York Minster. The pub next door, the Hole in the Wall (a reference to Bootham Bar?), was once called the Board Inn. Excavations of the Board Inn in 1816 revealed a dark secret: a hole was discovered which led to a dungeon with chains and manacles on the walls. A tunnel was also found that had been bricked up.

Coffee Yard is the longest Snickelway at nearly 220ft (67m), leading off Stonegate; there you can find a reconstructed mediaeval townhouse, Barley Hall, which was originally built in about 1360 by the monks of Nostell Priory, a monastery near Wakefield.

Pope's Head Alley, measuring only 80cm wide, is one of the narrowest and darkest of York's streets.

Three Cranes Lane leads from Swinegate to St Sampson's Square, which was once called Thursday Market.

Finkle Street, leading from St. Sampson's Square to Swinegate, comes from the Anglo-Saxon word for Crooked Street, 'Winkel'. It was also once known as Mucky Pig Lane for its associations with the pig market.

Lady Peckett's Yard, Connects Fossgate with Pavement and is named after the wife of John Peckett, a Lord Mayor of York. It was called Bacusgail (Bake House Lane) in 1312 and later housed an auctioneers and Richardson's, a money lender. In 1857 Joseph Rowntree II rented a building in the yard for one of his adult schools where they taught men to read and write using scripture lessons; women followed soon after. Mary Kitching was president of the 'B' class of Lady Peckett's Yard Ladies' School for 14 years, until in 1892 she left for missionary work in the Holy Land. A lion from a circus in Parliament Street escaped and was eventually cornered here in the early 1900s. Nearby in Black Horse Passage, Joseph Rowntree set up a soup kitchen in 1845. The nearby Golden Fleece pub has named one of its rooms Lady Peckett's Room.

Bedern Passage, a snickelway off Goodramgate, leads to Bedern Lane and the remains of Bedern Chapel, which was consecrated in 1349 as the Chapel of the College of the Vicars Choral of York Minster. The chapel was the centre of a large monastic-like complex where the mediaeval vicars lived and worked.

Narrow Lop Lane or Little Blake Street, accessed through Peter Gate, was widened in 1860 and 1864 to form Duncombe Place and a vista of the Minster. Etridge's Royal Hotel, a coaching inn, was in Blake Street, demolished in 1859 for the York Poor Law Union.

69

Colliergate Drill Hall

A beautiful polychromatic brick building

The impressive polychromatic brick doorway. At the centre of the low one-storey range is a double wooden door, nicely chamfered, with a pair of slim pilasters either side, complete with tiny leafy capitals, and a very attractive tile-patterned pediment. This features the white rose of York, surrounded by a pattern of stylised bay leaves in the outer part of the arch.

Colliergate Drill Hall was designed in the late 19th century by Gould and Fisher for the 1st West Yorkshire (York) Rifle Battalion, which evolved to become the The Prince of Wales's Own Regiment of Yorkshire in 1881 and the 5th Battalion The Prince of Wales's Own Regiment of Yorkshire in 1908. Elements of the 5th Battalion, the West Yorkshire Regiment, continued to use the drill hall until the battalion amalgamated with the 4th Battalion, the East Yorkshire Regiment, to form the 3rd Battalion the Prince of Wales's Own Regiment of Yorkshire in 1960. After the new battalion was established at Lumley Barracks in York, the Colliergate Drill Hall was decommissioned and has since been converted for use by Barnitt's hardware store.

The inscription above the doorway reads 'Pro aris et focis' – 'For our altars and our homes'. It is a beautiful, sadly overlooked, building, but now happily listed. The doorway is faced with polychromatic brick – unusual in York, and only seen elsewhere in the city on Trinity Chapel, Peckitt Street, at the fire station. It was a house in the early 19th century, converted to an inn later that century and adapted for military use 1872, retaining the mid-19th-century inn front, and with the drill hall added on to the stableyard.

70

The Printer's Devil, Stonegate

The Printers' Devil glowering down on Stonegate. Image courtesy of Visit York; © Jim Richardson; thanks to Sarah Foster, Communications Manager.

Printing came to England in 1477 with William Caxton and is first recorded in York soon after in 1497 when Fridericus Freez, an immigrant 'docheman', is noted as 'Book Bynder' and 'Stationer' and later as a 'Buke Printer'. Hugo Goez set up in 1509 and in 1642 the King's Printer worked out of St William's College, beneath the majestic East Window. Thomas Gent (d. 1778) published scores of chap books from Coffee Yard. Grace White was the first woman to publish a newspaper here in 1718, *The York Mercury*, with Thomas Hammond, Quaker bookseller and publisher; the paper passed to Thomas Gent in 1724.

Minerva, at the top of Stonegate. Roman goddess of learning, she is another symbol of the bookish character of this part of York where publishing, printing and bookselling once thrived.

See:

Chrystal, Paul, *The Book: How the Wisdom of the Classical World Was Preserved: Writing, Publishing & Bookselling,* Barnsley, 2023.

Chrystal, Paul, *York Places of Learning,* Stroud, 2011.

Sessions, William, K. *Printing in York from the 1490s to the Present Day,* York, 1976.

71

The Hospitium

A mediaeval guest house for tradesmen visitors to the Abbey

The Hospitium today.

People often ask what this building was, and is. A splendid 14th-century half-timbered building in Museum Gardens, it was probably designed both as a guest house for 'lower rank' visitors to the nearby St Mary's Abbey (merchants for example) and as a warehouse for goods for the abbey, conveniently unloaded from the river nearby. Its name derives from our 'hospitality', rather than 'hospital' and, as noted, was built as a place to house and feed visiting pilgrims. The Hospitium originally formed part of a group of buildings in the abbey grounds that included a brew-house, stables, mill and, near the main gate, a boarding school for 50 pupils. The ruined gateway at the side dates back to the 15th century, and was probably the entrance to a passage that ran towards a water-gate by the river. An Elizabethan knot garden with central fountain lay between the Hospitium and the river.

Over the years it has had a number of different uses: early images show it was used as a farm building; in the 19th century, the Yorkshire Philosophical Society repaired the building and used it to display museum objects. In the 1930s the upper storey was extended and a new roof put in place. In 2008, for the first time, running water, toilets, a passenger lift and a kitchen were installed. The building is now the jewel of York Museum Trust's hospitality business and is a popular venue for weddings and fairs.

The knot garden and fountain

72

The All Saints Pavement Doom Knocker

Knock on the doom knocker before entering

The doom knocker

Before you can get into this church you have to get past the 12th century 'doom knocker' on the north door; it is a bronze sanctuary ring depicting, in god-fearing detail, a bearded man, a sinner, being devoured by a lion – the mouth of hell. The original is in the York Minster Treasury. All Saints can boast a somewhat gruesome relic – the plate on which John the Baptist's decapitated head was presented to Herod; another indication perhaps of the church's high status in mediaeval days.

In common with other churches and buildings in the city, All Saints is infested with mice – six of Robert Thompson's familiar wood-carved rodents are to be found in the church. They are kept company by a number of carved green men.

The regimental window.

All Saints is the Guild and Civic church of York and the Regimental church of the Royal Dragoon Guards. Thirty-four York Lord Mayors are buried here. In 2015 the poignant Afghanistan Memorial Window was installed.

The Doom Stone at York Minster

On a similar theme, the Doom Stone at York Minster is, appropriately, in the crypt, is a hellish relief from the 12th century which depicts a

The Doom Stone.

cauldron into which the souls of the damned are being shoved and tortured by terrifying demons. Above the cauldron, a elegantly dressed woman symbolises luxury, and two figures with heavy purses around their necks represent avarice. In addition, two demons and two devils who support the cauldron hold a tortured soul in the flames. To the right of the cauldron are three mouths of hell.

73

The Afghanistan Memorial Window

A memorial to the three York servicemen who made the ultimate sacrifice

In July 2015 a very special event took place in the church: the unveiling of the Afghanistan 2001–14 window in which three fallen soldiers from York are commemorated, along with the many other York citizens who served there. One of the country's premier stained-glass artists, Helen Whittaker of Barley Studios in Dunnington near York, installed the window.

It was funded by the City of York Afghanistan Commemorative Appeal, which was launched by *The Press* in 2011 and has raised more than £17,000.

To recognise the city's sons and daughters who answered the call of duty in Afghanistan, and provide a memorial to the three York servicemen who made the ultimate sacrifice: Marine David Hart, Trooper Ashley David Smith and Lance Bombardier Matthew Hatton. Helen said the main focus of the window design was the traditional symbol of peace in the form of a dove, which was also the symbol of the Holy Spirit… Regiments which had lost men serving in Afghanistan: the Royal Dragoon Guards (maroon, gold and green), the 40th Regiment Royal Artillery (red and blue) and the Royal Marines (blue, red, green and yellow)… The three York servicemen are represented as individual sets, proudly displaying their regimental badges, and flying upwards towards the heavenly City, a golden circular light beneath the dove, that illuminates the path of those no longer with us. The yellow colour also reminds us of the sun and desert earth of Afghanistan.

The splendid window.

74

York's Barnbow Canaries

'The only memorial in the country to the women of the British Empire who lost their lives during the First World War'

Barnbow Canaries 1918 celebrating the end of the war.

Barnbow Munitions Factory – National Filling Factory No. 1 was a World War One munitions factory located between Cross Gates and Garforth in Leeds. Sadly, Barnbow is best known for the massive explosion that killed 35 of the women workers one night in 1916.

Barnbow was always a very dangerous place to work. Workers who handled the explosives stripped to their underwear, and wore smocks, puttees, caps, rubber gloves and rubber soled boots to avoid sparks; cigarettes and matches were obviously banned, except in safe areas, as were combs and hairpins to prevent static electricity. Workers were allowed to drink as much barley water and milk as they liked and, to help with the milk, Barnbow had its own farm, with a herd of 120 cows producing 300 gallons of milk per day. As we know, working with cordite turns the skin yellow – the only known antidote was milk. Because of the yellowness of the women's skin, they were called 'The Barnbow Canaries'.

Women were bussed in from far and wide to work shifts at Barnbow, including York. On Tuesday, 5 December 1916, 170 women and girls had just started their night shift in one of the fusing rooms: 4½-inch shells were being filled, fused and packed in Room 42 when the explosion took place. Many of the dead were only identifiable by their identity disks. The injured were taken to Leeds General Infirmary with the help of the factory medical staff, the ambulance corps and the voluntary motor transport section. Production was interrupted only for a short time, and once the bodies were recovered, other girls immediately volunteered to replace them in Room 42.

Apart from setting up a dignified memorial, in 2012 the people of Leeds named a number of parks, buildings and streets in memory of the 'Barnbow Lasses'. The names of those who died are listed in the roll of honour in Colton Methodist Church, and in York Minster near to the Five Sisters Window. Louise Birch, from Leeds Central Library, has researched some very tragic and moving details about the casualties, as given in her 'Remembering the Barnbow Tragedy: 100 Years Ago Today' (https://secretlibraryleeds.net/tag/barnbow/). Here are the stories of two casualties from York:

> **Mary E. Carter of York**, died aged 22 (*Yorkshire Herald*, 16 December 1916): *Women patriot's funeral at York of soldier's young wife… The funeral took place at York cemetery yesterday of Mary Elizabeth Carter, aged 22, daughter of Mr and Mrs Eshelby, 3, Fettergate-lane, Micklegate, York, and wife of Lance-Corporal W. Carter, who met her death last week under tragic circumstances. There is one child, aged two years. A brother is serving in France… She was formerly employed at Messrs. Rowntree's factory. There were pathetic scenes at the funeral, which was largely attended, a number of the deceased's fellow-workers heading the cortege.*

Olive Yeates of York: Olive was survived by three children and a husband with tuberculosis. Rumours handed down by survivors reported that Olive was working on the shell that exploded. Today, Olive Yeates Way on the old Barnbow site is named in her honour.

The Five Sisters Memorial in York Minster honours local munitions workers who died in service, including Barnbow girls and women. Astonishingly, this is the only memorial in the country to the women of the British Empire who lost their lives during the World War One. The names of the 1,400 women commemorated are inscribed on oak screens on the north side of the St Nicholas's Chapel. This memorial lists by far the greatest number of names of any in the minster or cathedral, including that of Edith Cavell, the British nurse executed by a German firing squad in 1915.

See:

Paul Chrystal, *Leeds's Military Heritage*, 2017.

Paul Chrystal, *Women at Work in World War I and II*, Barnsley, 2023.

75

Soviet rocket – a Big Hit in York

...to 'provoke and inspire' staff (!)

The motivational rocket (courtesy of York Press).

Some of the more than 900 pieces of artwork went on display at the annual Twitter Art Exhibition charity event, which in 2022 was held in York's 2016 four-storey 4,432m² block Hiscox Building in Peaseholme Green. A decommissioned Soviet rocket (Soviet S-200) is the centrepiece for this sculptural cast-concrete office designed by Make Architects for insurance company Hiscox. The website tells us:

> *The 12-metre-long decommissioned rocket sits at the centre of the atrium, illuminated from above by a curving skylight. It is one of several artworks integrated into the office, intended to 'provoke and inspire' staff.*
> - www.dezeen.com/2016/02/19/make-architects-hiscox-office-building-york-soviet-rocket/

The S-200 **(NATO: SA-5 Gammon)** is a Russian medium to high-altitude surface-to-air missile (SAM) system. A highly proliferated weapon, it is nuclear capable and currently in service in at least 12 countries including Russia, North Korea and Ukraine.

According to https://missilethreat.csis.org/defsys/s-200-sa-5-gammon:

On October 4, 2001, the Ukrainian military accidentally shot down Siberia Airlines Flight 1812 flying from Tel Aviv to Novosibirsk. As part of an air defense exercise, two antiair missiles, one from an S-200 and one from an S-300, were launched at a target drone off the Black Sea's Crimean coast. The missile from the S-300 successfully intercepted the drone, but the errant S-200 missile flew an extra 240 km before hitting a Russian Tu-154 commercial airliner.

The plane was hit while flying 35,000ft above the Black Sea, killing all 78 crew and passengers.

76

The Baedeker Raid, 1942

The raids on York, Norwich, Bath, Canterbury and Exeter became known as Baedeker Raids because Goring's staff allegedly used the famous travel guide to select their *Vergeltungsangriffe* (retaliatory) targets – namely 3*** English cities – in retaliation for the RAF's destruction of Lübeck and Rostock. Following the nine-month blitz on London and other cities, Britain had responded with a ferocious and deadly attack on Lübeck in March 1942. In a change of tactics, an Area Bombing Directive was issued to the RAF on 14 February 1942, authorising the targeting of civilian areas. Deploying the new *Wellington* and *Stirling* heavy bombers, Lübeck was blanket bombed; blockbuster bombs were followed by 25,000 incendiary devices, creating a massive firestorm. The city was devastated and hundreds of civilians were killed. Lübeck had been targeted as it was lightly defended and had a large number of mediaeval timber buildings which would ignite easily. Hitler 'shared [Goebbels's] opinion absolutely that cultural centres, health resorts and civilian centres must be attacked ... there is no other way of bringing the English to their senses. They belong to a class of human beings with whom you can only talk after you have first knocked out their teeth.' (Terraine p. 479.)

Seventy German bombers, largely unopposed, bombed York for two hours, beginning at 2.30am and finishing 90 minutes later – although the official all-clear was not given until 4.46am. In total, 84 tonnes of bombs were dropped, together with clusters of incendiary devices, and German planes dive-bombed streets, strafing them with machine-gun fire. Ninety-four people died including 14 children, and 98 were seriously injured (not including undisclosed army and RAF fatalities). Allied planes shot down four enemy aircraft; 9,500 houses (30 per cent of the city's stock) were damaged or destroyed, leaving 2,000 people homeless. The Guildhall and St Martin le Grand Church were badly damaged. The Bar Convent School collapsed, killing five nuns including the headmistress, Mother Vincent. The Carriageworks roundhouse took a direct hit and all of the 20 engines in there at the time suffered damage. *The Sir Ralph Wedgwood* A4 Pacific (named after the former NER Chief General Manager) was totally destroyed when a bomb blew up in Clifton engine shed.

The Sir Ralph Wedgwood A4 Pacific written off (courtesy of York Press).

The following day the *Daily Mail* reported: 'The gates of York still stand high, like the spirit of its people who, after nearly two hours of intense bombing and machine-gunning, were clearing up today.' There is a plaque on York Railway Station in honour of Station Foreman William Milner who died in the raid while entering a burning building to get medical supplies. His body was found still holding the box; he was posthumously awarded the King's Commendation for Gallantry.

77

Pilot Officer Yves Mathé

Free French fighter pilot.

We have much to thank a young French pilot for; Yves Mahé played a crucial role in the defence of York that Baedeker night and prevented further damage, death and destruction in the city below.

Yves Mahé was born in Nantes, Loire-Atlantique, France, on 21 November 1919. He qualified as a civilian pilot and then joined the French Air Force. During World War Two, as German troops advanced and the French Third Republic signed the Armistice with Germany on 20 June 1940, Yves joined the Free French Forces and, travelling on a stolen plane, first to Gibraltar then on to England, he was reunited with his brother, also a pilot.

By April 1942, at the age of 23, Yves was serving with 253 (Hyderabad) Squadron, RAF Fighter Command, which had returned from the Orkneys in late 1941 to be based in Lincolnshire, flying convoy protection off the east coast. York Civic trust website provides the detail:

> *Four RAF stations were tasked with defending York including RAF Hibaldstow where 253 Squadron had a number of Free French Air Force pilots. Flying his* Hawker Hurricane II, *Yves Mahé saw the city of York ablaze from a distance so set off alone with all eight machine guns blazing and shot down a* Heinkel HIII *bomber in flames over the River Ouse. The bombers had been lining up to attack the main Rowntree factory but then retreated. Although Yves received support from other aircraft which followed, his lone intervention had set the attackers in retreat.*
>
> *The young pilot was given a civic reception at the Mansion House in York. Later General de Gaulle presented him with the Croix de Guerre. He went on to fly with French air squadrons, fighting with the Soviet Air Force and was shot down over Smolensk in 1944. He was captured by the Germans, condemned to death but escaped.*
>
> *He served with the French air force until 1962 when he was killed flying a* Gloster Meteor *jet night fighter which crashed in Belgium. He was 42.*

See:

Chrystal, Paul, *A History of Chocolate in York*, Barnsley, 2012.

Kessler, Leo (Charles Whiting), and Taylor, Eric, *The York Blitz, 1942: The Baedeker Raid on York*, York, 1986.

Rothnie, Niall, *The Baedeker Blitz*, Ian Allan, 1992.

Terraine, John, *The Right of the Line*, Hodder & Stoughton, 1985.

https://raidsoveryork.co.uk/raid8-29-apr-1942/

78

Bettys Dive and that Mirror

Many of the signatories did not survive the war

Waitress Pam Broadbent giving the mirror a polish on 8 October 1993 (courtesy of York Press).

On 1 February 1945, JE McDonald was the first of 600 airmen to scratch their names on the mirror at Bettys in York during World War Two ('J.E. MacDonald 1-2-45'). Also variously known as Bettys Bar, The Dive and the Briefing Room, it was a regular haunt of the hundreds of airmen stationed in and around York; these included many Canadians from Number 6 Bomber Group. One signatory, Jim Rogers, borrowed a waitress's diamond ring to scratch his name on the mirror. Many have returned to reflect on their courageous experiences at the mirror, which is on display downstairs in Bettys; many of the signatories did not survive the war.

We maintain that we provide an essential public service in York and we sincerely hope that you will not find it necessary to commandeer the establishment.

For a list of signatories see:
https://425alouette.wordpress.com/2017/01/13/bettys-bar/

The striking ice sculpture outside Bettys during the 2023 York Ice Trail. The train symbolises the city's strong railway heritage as well as its strong associations with confectionery.

Who was Betty?

So who really was Betty? The true identity of Betty has never been revealed and almost certainly never will be. Speculation is rife, however, and there have been many claimants. She may have been the daughter of a doctor who practised in the building in Cambridge Crescent, which was to become the Harrogate Bettys, and who died from tuberculosis; she could have been Betty Lupton, celebrated Queen of the Harrogate Wells from 1778–1838 and chief 'nymph'; she might also have been the actress Betty Fairfax who starred in the West End musical *Betty* around 1915 and to whom owner Frederick Belmont took something of a shine; intriguingly, the musical toured the country and came to Harrogate's Grand Opera House three times between 1916 and 1918. Or, just as plausibly, Betty may be the name of the little girl who brought in a toy tea tray during a meeting at which the name for the new cafe was being discussed…

See:

Gray, Annie, *From the Alps to the Dales: 100 Years of Bettys*, Profile, 2019.

Chrystal, Paul, *A History of Chocolate in York*, Barnsley, 2012.

Chrystal, Paul, *Confectionery in Yorkshire*, Stroud, 2012.

Wild, J, *Hearts, Tarts & Rascals*, Harrogate, 2010.

79

Constantine the Great

The Emperor Constantine is a key figure in what is essentially one of Britain's foremost Roman cities. We are used to seeing him resplendent in Philip Jackson's bronze outside the Minster wielding his broken sword. Here he is, though, in a very different setting: he is outside the Yorkshire Museum, cast in ice, as part of the splendid 2023 York Ice Trail.

On becoming emperor in AD 305, Constantius launched a successful punitive campaign against the Picts beyond the Antonine Wall. However, he died suddenly in Eboracum (York) in 306. Before he did, however, Constantius recommended his son to the influential army as his successor; consequently Constantine was declared emperor by the legions at York. He went on to establish the foundations of Roman Christendom in Britain.

Constantine in ice, York Ice Trail, February 2023.

Constantine in bronze outside the Minster, which is built on top of his fortress.

The emperor Constantine died in York in 337 – the first emperor to adopt the Christian faith , beginning the ending of the persecution of Christians in the Roman Empire in what was known as the Triumph of the Church, the Peace of the Church or the Constantinian Shift. In 313, Constantine and Licinius issued the Edict of Milan decriminalising Christian worship throughout the Roman empire. Religious tolerance, of a sort, had arrived.

80

Alicia Thornton

Britain's 'first female jockey'

Alicia Thornton by Mackenzie, after unknown artist stipple engraving, published 1805 (NPG D8248 © National Portrait Gallery, London) by J. Wheble, Warwick Square, by Mackenzie and Pierce Egan's Book of Sports.

Alicia Thornton or Alicia Meynel (1780s–1800s) can claim to be the 'first female jockey' after she took part in a horse race at what is now York Racecourse on Knavesmire in August 1804.

Alicia first attracted attention in 1804 when she challenged a man to a horse race that man was her neighbour and brother-in-law Captain William Flint. Alicia's husband, Colonel Thomas Thornton, offered her his horse and placed a bet on her winning. The prize was either 500 guineas (or 1,500 guineas). Thornton later said he believed it was 500 guineas and he had only mentioned the 1,500 figure to attract a crowd.

It was said that 100,000 people watched and placed bets as she, riding Vinagrillo side saddle, 'displayed great ability in the management of her horse and kept the lead nearly the whole race'. Some say that her saddle worked loose and that her horse became lame. Whatever, sadly Mrs Thornton came second, but 'her striking attire, spirited acceptance of the wager, skill and courage, coupled with her admirable good humour in defeat, made her a favourite of the crowd and long-celebrated even after the race was concluded'. Colonel Thornton came away with a reputation for being a bit eccentric for 'turning his Lady into a racing jockey'. Victory, though, came the following year for Alicia when she won on Louisa, again at the Knavesmire.

See:

Brailsford, Dennis, 'Thornton [Meynell], Alicia (fl. 1804), horsewoman, Oxford Dictionary of National Biography', *Oxford Dictionary of National Biography* (online ed.), Oxford University Press.

81

The Workhouse

'We found a Beast's Head at that time offensive to the smell... a quantity of unwholesome mucus was attached to it.'

Some of the nurses at the York workhouse about 1920.

In 1551, part of St Anthony's Hall, one of York's Houses of Correction at the time, was used as a poorhouse. In 1567 and 1569, two weaving establishments were set up for the unemployed in St Anthony's Hall and St George's House, but the goods they produced were useless. After many unsuccessful attempts, a number of the city's parishes set up a joint workhouse in 1768 to accommodate 90 paupers in a former cotton factory at 26 Marygate, again, working with textiles.

York Poor Law Union was established in 1837 and took over Marygate: hygiene left much to be desired, according to this 1839 inspection, triggered after an outbreak of food poisoning from a vat of soup:

> *In a room, however, in my opinion as a Chemist, ill adapted for the purpose of preserving meat, we found a Beast's Head at that time offensive to the smell… This room adjoins and opens into a short and very narrow yard considerably tainted with all the effluvia rising from some privies at one end ... The head not having been previously cleaned, a quantity of unwholesome mucus was attached to it.*

The Guardians nevertheless concluded that the soup had made inmates ill because 'the usual quantity of Potatos [sic] had been omitted making the soup too strong and rich'. The Poor Law Commissioners recommended a replacement for the Marygate workhouse reporting 'a permanent reservoir of foul air', and the privies were 'without exception in an offensive state'.

Most of the inmates were 'children, the aged and infirm and persons of weak mind'; many, if not all, were diseased and children mixed 'in the infectious wards with adults labouring under syphilis and gonorrhea'. The paupers mocked the idiots 'as a pastime'. In August 1845, the *Leeds Mercury* reported on the women's ward in an official inspection: 'this place is used by aged idiots, women and children, and besides being of limited extent, it has only one privy, with an open cesspool.' In 1849 a new union workhouse was built on Huntington Road, housing 300 inmates. Different inmates were separated by a network of walls, including one specifically for unmarried women and one for 'female idiots'. There was also a washhouse, laundry, and the mortuary. On the men's side were an oakum-picking shop, carpenter's shop, stone yard, and a coach house. In 1930, the workhouse became a Public Assistance Institution, while part of the building was affiliated to York City Hospital. In 1946 it was renamed the Grange, and in 1955 became St Mary's Hospital. This closed in the late 1970s and the buildings were converted to student accommodation.

See:

www.workhouses.org.uk/York/

82

Eden Camp Modern History Museum

This full size replica of a Hawker Hurricane greets you at Eden Camp (P2793 Eden Camp Modern History Theme Museum BAPC236 'SD-M' full-size model).

The Hawker Hurricane is a British single-seat fighter aircraft of the 1930s–40s which was designed and predominantly built by Hawker Aircraft Ltd for service with the Royal Air Force (RAF). It was overshadowed in the public consciousness by the Supermarine Spitfire during the Battle of Britain in 1940, but the Hurricane inflicted 60 percent of the losses sustained by the Luftwaffe in the engagement, and fought in all the major theatres of the Second World War.
https://www.baesystems.com/en-uk/heritage/hurricane

Eden Camp (PW Work Camp 83) is a family run and owned museum near Malton. It started life in 1942 as a temporary Prisoner of War camp, with barbed wire and tents to accommodate Italian prisoners of war captured in North Africa. Local businessman Stan Johnson bought the site and initially invested £750,000 to create, within the original camp, the world's only Modern History Theme Museum.

Back in the 1940s, its first residents were 250 Italian prisoners escorted from Oldham and marched through Malton to their new home where they got to work on constructing a larger and more permanent camp.

At its peak, Eden Camp's 45 huts and tented accommodation could accommodate around 1,200 prisoners. In summer 1944, the Italian prisoners, after Italy had surrendered, gave way to Polish soldiers mustered for the invasion of Europe and then to German POWs. The Germans, like the Italians before them, were mainly put to work locally in agriculture until 1948–1949, when they were finally released.

Stan Johnson bought the site intending to set up a potato crisp factory. But when three Italian ex-Eden Camp prisoners of war approached him seeking permission to look around the camp, the innovative idea of preserving the camp and opening it as a museum was born.

The Camp website tells us that:

> *The huts have been re-equipped to tell the story of The People's War, the social history of life in Britain from 1939 to 1945. Realistic tableaux, with moving figures, authentic sounds and smells, have been created to 'transport you back in time'. Each hut covers a different aspect of the war, starting with the rise of the Nazi Party, Hitler and The Outbreak of War. Other topics include: Rationing, the Utility Scheme, 'Save It' Campaigns, Evacuees, Propaganda, Home Guard, Home Front, The Blitz, Air Raid and Gas Precautions, Animals at War, The Street at War, Women at War, The Land Army and Timber Girls, The Munition Factories, The Observer Corps, The Auxiliary Fire Service, The WVS, The Red Cross, Civil Defence, The Rescue Services, The Bevin Boys and more.*

In 2022, following the pandemic, the museum spent ¼ million pounds refurbishing the camp and the new Blitz Experience opened.

See:

Chrystal, Paul, *From the Northwest Frontier to Stalag 383: The Experiences of a Seaforth Highlander in World War II*, Barnsley, 2023.

Whittaker, Adam, 'Technically Creative to modernise classic UK attraction, Eden Camp' *Blooloop*, 19 November 2021.

83

Poor Clare Colettines Nuns

Mother Abbess to the Pope: 'it's only bricks and mortar,' she said

Essential produce from the Poor Clares (courtesy of York Press).

The first 40 sisters came to York from Bruges at the instigation of Marcia, Lady Herries of Everingham Hall, near Market Weighton. Originally called the Poor Ladies, the order was founded at Assisi, in central Italy, by Clare (1193/4–1253), a noblewoman who became a disciple of Francis of Assisi (1181/2–1226). The first convent of the Sisters of the Second Order of Saint Francis was Plantation House in Hull Road in 1865; they moved to the enclosed five acre St Joseph's Monastery in Lawrence Street in 1873.

In mediaeval England, the nuns were known as 'Minoresses' and their principal monastery, the Abbey of the Order of St Clare, was near Aldgate in London. The order gave its name to the street still known as Minories on the eastern boundary of the City. Until recently they lived in York's St Joseph's behind 20ft high walls, got up at 5.00am, lived in silence, were vegetarians and cultivated a six-acre garden to make themselves largely self-sufficient. At its height during the 1940s, the convent was home to more than 40 nuns. The convent comprised cloisters, cells, chapel and refectory.

The remaining eight Poor Clare Colettines have now moved to a house in Askham Bryan. The convent's Mother Abbess sought permission from the Vatican for the move and admitted to mixed feelings: 'it's only bricks and mortar,' she said.

The convent has been converted into student accommodation, Vita. Some vestiges of the building's former life remain and the grass in the old orchard has been sensitively cut in the shape of a cross.

The simple and austere nature of the building's architecture and internal decorative schemes was untouched, providing a tangible illustration of rare monastic architecture and how the nuns would have lived their entire lives within an enclosed order... the new development within the landscape respected historic character areas and boundaries. Retention of the high enclosure walls, the nun's burial ground and garden areas, such as the orchard, was crucial to a sensitive scheme.

- www.purcelluk.com/discover/vita-student-project-at-st-josephs-convent-york-shortlisted-for-riba-awards/

See:

Chrystal, Paul, *Changing York,* Stroud, 2015.

Chrystal, Paul, *York's Churches & Places of Worship*, Catrine, 2017.

Knox, Lezlie, 'Poor Clares Order', *Women and Gender in Medieval Europe, An Encyclopaedia,* Margaret C Shaus (ed), Routledge, 2006.

84

4468 Mallard

A painting of Mallard features on the 1993 Blur album Modern Life Is Rubbish.

Fireman Jim Fletcher and 17 former Mallard drivers celebrate 30 years of the engine's retirement in 1963 in York's National Railway Museum where the resplendent locomotive resides (courtesy of York Press).

LNER 4468 *Mallard* is a LNER Class A4 4-6-2 steam locomotive built by the London & North Eastern Railway at Doncaster Works in 1938. It is the holder of the world speed record for steam locomotives at 126 mph (203 km/h). The A4 class was designed by Nigel Gresley; *Mallard* covered almost one and a half million miles (2.4 million km).

See:

Chrystal, Paul, *York and its Railways 1839–1950,* Catrine, 2015.

85

King's Manor Coat of Arms

Catherine Howard came with him [Henry VIII] to York in 1541 and allegedly consummated her affair with Thomas Culpepper in the rose garden

The splendid King's Manor coat of arms.

This magnificent, often overlooked, building off Exhibition Square, was originally built in 1270 as the house of the Abbott at St Mary's Abbey. It was rebuilt in 1480 – the new windows providing the earliest known examples of the use of terracotta as a building material. The Dissolution of the Monasteries was nothing if not selective and pragmatic: the Manor was retained by the Crown and allocated to the Council of the North. It became the official residence of the President of the Council in 1561 and was gradually enlarged and extended westwards with much of the building work completed during the reign of Elizabeth I. Visitors included Henry VIII and James I; during the Siege of York in 1644 it was the Royalists' headquarters. Henry VIII's Hidden Vaults lie under the King's Manor, and it is speculated that the long sought after Roman colosseum is under there too. Catherine Howard, fifth wife of Henry VIII, came with him to York in 1541 and allegedly consummated her affair with Thomas Culpepper in the rose garden of the King's Manor.

The ornate doorway with the stunning coat of arms at the main entrance is Jacobean; the 'IR' signifies James I, who ordered the Manor be converted into a royal palace for him to stay in on his journeys to and from London and Edinburgh. After a long period of private lettings and decay, Mr Lumley's Boarding School for Ladies occupied it from 1712–1835 and then the William Wilberforce-inspired Yorkshire School for the Blind moved in, in 1833, and, from the 1870s, gradually restored and enlarged the buildings, adding a gymnasium and a cloister to create a second courtyard. The Blind School left in 1958; the Manor was then acquired by York City Council, who leased it to the University of York in 1963 when it was used to house the Institute for Advanced Architectural Studies. In 1997, the main occupant was the Department of Archaeology (including the Archaeology Data Service), plus the Centre for Mediaeval Studies and the Centre for Eighteenth Century Studies.

See:

RCHME Inventory of the City of York, Volume IV.

86

Terry's Clock

This fascinating image of Terry's famous clock from inside and behind the face, taken during redevelopment of the building, is courtesy of Tassadar@ midlandsheritageforum.

Knighted in 1936, Sir Francis Terry was an enigmatic character. He would often bring in flowers from the garden for the office girls; quality, though, could never be compromised. Peter Terry relates the story of Sir Francis officiating at a tasting session one day when he exclaimed, 'I have never seen such stuff!' and threw the samples out of the open window to be gathered up later by ground staff. On the other hand he could show real generosity: for the trip to London to receive his knighthood, all the employees' works numbers were put in a hat and 12 were drawn out; these lucky dozen stayed at the Savoy and took in a show at the Drury Lane Theatre.

See:

Chrystal, Paul, *A History of Chocolate in York, Barnsley,* 2012.

Chrystal, Paul, *Confectionery in Yorkshire,* Stroud, 2012.

87

John Wilhelm Rowntree – Racist?

Mowgli Made Leader of the Bandar-Log.

John Charles Dollman (1851–1934), Shipley Art Gallery, Gateshead.

This painting is based on the Rudyard Kipling story 'Kaa's Hunting', collected in The Jungle Book. The painting depicts Mowgli in the Cold Lairs, an abandoned human city taken over by the Bandar-Log (Monkey Folk). The monkeys have promised to make Mowgli their leader, claiming that as a human raised by animals he can demonstrate his human wisdom to them. Soon, however, he learns that they only consider him an amusing toy and are already growing bored of him.

John Wilhelm Rowntree was born on 4 September 1868 at Top House, York, the first child of Joseph Rowntree Snr and Emma Antoinette. He was chocolate magnate Joseph Rowntree's brother.

In 1898 John Wilhelm travelled to the Caribbean and Mexico, New Orleans and Chicago with his wife, Constance. His exploits were recorded, somewhat reluctantly, in his journal 'on this floating temple of indolence [*The Aratro,* where] good resolves melt like butter ... I was reported alive but unconscious'. Constance, an occasional surrogate journalist, confirms the otiose lifestyle: 'John has developed such a capacity for laziness ... he will just write a postscript to correct all my erroneous statements' (*S. Allott, John Wilhelm Rowntree* (York, 1994) pp. 56ff.

Describing a mix of chocolate business and sightseeing, the Mexico diaries are fascinating, if at times somewhat disturbing: *the 'copper coloured' coolies were comely women to look at, small and graceful, and with such a carriage... [with]strikingly refined faces in sharp contrast to chattering wooly-pated niggers with their coarse features, obtrusive manners, and overflowing conceit. The nigger is to the white what the Banderlog were to the jungle... they are hopelessly incompetent, incorrigibly idle, overpowering in their conceit and more effervescent than the Parisians... They are, however, very picturesque and the women ... carry themselves magnificently and walk like Greek Goddesses.*

Allott quotes more: *Banderlog monkeys feature in Kipling's The Jungle Book. 'Bander' is a Hindi word, a term to denote 'Langur monkeys'; 'log' means 'people'. They appear in the tale of Kaa's Hunting, where they are ostracised by the other animals on account of their garrulous stupidity; there anthem is 'We are great. We are free. We are wonderful. We are the most wonderful people in all the jungle! We all say so, and so it must be true'. Banderlogs communicate by mimicking other animals' speech.*

Copies were sent to Frank Rowntree 'with instructions for it to be read to Acomb Adult School on the Sunday following receipt'. John Wilhelm's use of the word 'nigger' may not have been quite as offensive then as it is to modern ears. It was, though, being used in a pejorative sense from around 1900; despite this, advertisers, for example, continued to use it for some time after. There is no mitigation, however, for the comparison with Banderlogs.

In Chicago racial discrimination was there for all to see; John Wilhelm's reaction on seeing race-segregated waiting rooms is tinged with irony and inconsistent with the above, to say the least:

> *I suppose coloured people are never ladies and gentlemen. It is strange that, an Englishman, from a benighted country which still supports such a medieval institution as a monarchy, should find my first sentiment on the Republican and free soil of the States to be one of indignation at the insulting inequality and injustice to a coloured race who are yet, on paper, free and equal citizens with the whites.*

Quoted in S. Allott, *John Wilhelm Rowntree* (York, 1994,pp. 57ff).

See:

Chrystal, Paul, 'Rowntree Tales', in Stephen W. Angell, Quakers, Business, and Industry: Quakers and the Disciplines: Volume 4, *2017.*

Chrystal, Paul, The Rowntree family of York, 2013.

Allott, S, John Wilhelm Rowntree, 1994.

88

A Day in the Life in Bedern

'Get the whores out of Bedern'

Girls from St Stephen's Orphanage in York enjoying themselves on a day trip to Filey, July 1919 (courtesy of York Press).

By the 19th century, Bedern had become something a no-go area: in the 1820s and 1830s prostitution was rife. In 1839 13 brothel keepers were charged in one day for keeping bawdy houses; in 1843 the chief constable reported that, of York's 118 known prostitutes, 33 (28 per cent) lived in the Bedern. According to the police, there were seven brothels in Bedern in which 12 prostitutes plied their trade with another 12 or so under suspicion. In desperation, the police authorities asked the Ecclesiastical Commission to do something about it through the Vicars Choral. The following from the Commissioners illustrates the difficulty of bringing a viable prosecution:

> *Your petitioners three years ago, in order to get the whores out of it [Bedern]. Prosecuted one at great expense to the said Liberty, and with difficulty got evidence and a conviction for one month's imprisonment. At the expiration of that time, she went back in a cab or a fly, preceded by a band of music, and her associates flocked back double in number.*

The Commissioners also reported that the night patrolman had resigned 'in consequence of the insults he received and the continual destruction of his windows'. No one wanted the job.

The living conditions were amongst the worst in York at the time. Bedern was an unsavoury, violent and impoverished place with 300 people sharing just five toilets according to one report. On 10 October 1868, *The Yorkshire Gazette* reported on what was probably a typical day in Bedern with this encounter between John Rohan, Patrick Muldowney, Michael McMennamy and Bridget Rohan:

> *Complainant [McMennamy] went out of his own house… when John Rohan went behind him and struck him on the head with a poker… two girls were fighting at the same time… and notwithstanding the blow he tried to separate them and then Muldowney struck him with half a brick… and while prostrate Bridget went out with a rolling pin and gave him some rattlers on the head, and the others kicked him… John Rohan and Molly Rohan were also charged with assaulting Thomas McMennamy, son of the above-named complainant… the girl struck him with an iron bolt and also bit his finger.*

Bedern Hall

Bedern Hall was the first home of the 36 Vicars Choral of York Minster from 1349. The covered way was allowed by Richard II and made it easy for the vicars to get to the Minster, and to avoid the 'common people'. The present hall dates from 1370 and was used until 1650, after which time, in the 19th century, it became a 'sad spectacle of poverty and wretchedness' when divided into slum tenements, largely for Irish navvies.

The Gilds of Freemen, Master Builders and the Company of Cordwainers now occupy the hall, which was restored in 1984. Cordwainers worked in 'cordwan', a type of shoe leather named after the Spanish town of Cordoba, the principal mediaeval source of this leather. The 1272 Freemen's Rolls list over 200 Cordwainers here: the first entry is 'Thomas de Fulford, Cordwainer'. At the end of the 16th century, the gild's senior officials, known as Searchers, were empowered to inspect all leather and shoes coming into York, rejecting any they found to be of inferior quality.

See:

Chrystal, Paul, *York Churches & Places of Worship*, 2017.

89

The Vicars Choral…

…And their 'colourful nocturnal habits'

York Glaziers Trust, Bedern Workshop. York Glaziers Trust employees Kieran Muir (left) and Emily Price (right) remove a stained-glass window panel from the St Cuthbert Window at York Minster (photographs: Danny Lawson/PA wire).

In the pages on Bedern above, we saw how the Vicars Choral were called upon to help clean up the area, morally and socially. This piece may show that the very same Vicars Choral may not have had the best qualifications for the task and were probably not the best choice.

The collegiate buildings of the Vicars Choral lay east of the Minster across Goodramgate. Bedern Chapel was the first home of the 36 Vicars Choral of York Minster from 1349; they it was who sang in the Minster services. There were 36 Vicars Choral by 1300, one for each member of the chapter (the governing body of York Minster). The covered way here (some of which survives next to the National Trust shop) was allowed by Richard II and made it easy for the vicars to get to the Minster, and to avoid the 'common people'. The vicars in Bedern had been indulging in 'colourful nocturnal habits' and were re-housed in St William's College so that their behaviour could be monitored more closely. One incident involved a cathedral freelance hitting a man over the head with the blunt end of an axe.

Who exactly were the Vicars Choral? The day-to-day routine of worship in the Minster was the responsibility of the canons, whose appointment was in the gift of the King; sometimes their work took them away from the Minster so, in order to preserve the daily routine, deputies were appointed to take their place; these reserves had to be priests who could sing or chant and were known as Vicars Choral. Other responsibilities included saying masses for the souls of their dead patrons in the various Minster chantries. Regulations required them to live communally in a collegiate system.

Centuries-old stained glass featuring St Cuthbert has been returned to York Minster following conservation work BYT York Glazier's Trust. Panels of mediaeval glass are being restored as part of a £5m project, which began in March 2021.

The Minster's St Cuthbert Window dates from 1440 and tells the story of the life and miracles of one of northern England's most significant saints.

In total 152 panels, which make up the window, will be conserved during a five-year restoration scheme.

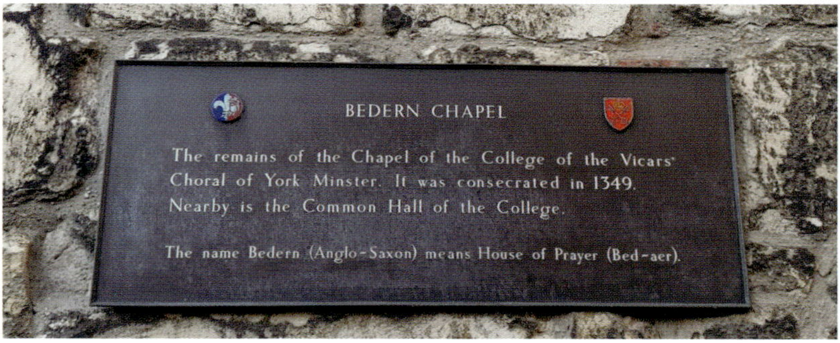

90

Sister Mary Xaveria and 'the Sound of Music'

her voice 'acted like magic on the undisciplined audience'.

Born in 1784, Sister Mary was a nun and a teacher at the Bar Convent and became Headmistress at the Poor School there in 1830. An earlier appointment was at St George's School in Walmgate where she taught 'a disorderly crowd of wild-looking little creatures for the most part barefooted , squalid and dirty, shouting and screaming'. Her solution was, in uncanny anticipation of Sister Maria in *The Sound of Music,* to sing, and her voice 'acted like magic on the undisciplined audience. In a few moments they were standing silent and almost motionless'.

Inside the wonderful Bar Convent.

91

'The Phoenix' and the Black Babies

'Your labour's in vain, black will never come white'

A superb collection of beer mats in the Phoenix.

The original name of this pub, until the mid-1800s, was 'The Labour in Vain'. The sign depicted a white woman vigorously scrubbing a black baby in a frantic bid to make it white; her labours, of course, were in vain. The inscription read 'You may wash him and scrub him from morn till night; your labour's in vain, black will never come white'.

Surprisingly perhaps, there are still a few pubs that have this name: one is in Yarnfield, Stone, in Staffordshire and another in Stourbridge in the West Midlands. Ann Jolly was the landlady of the York Labour in Vain/Black Boy in 1939; her husband, John Jolly, had run a pub on King's Staith, also called the Labour in Vain. When Ann Jolly died, the pub took the name the Black Boy, a reference to the black baby on the sign.

Today's more prosaic name derives from 1876 from the Phoenix Iron Foundry, which stood nearby before it moved in the mid-1870s to a new site on Leeman Road. The pub goes as far back as the late 18th century, although what you see inside now comes courtesy of a late 19th-century refit. The Phoenix Inn served the old cattle market, held behind Fishergate Bar until 1827.

See:

Chrystal, Paul, *Pubs in and Around York,* Destinworld, 2018.

92

The Iron Maiden

'used for the Incarceration of children in their orphanages'

The Spiked iron cage or the Iron Maiden: an upright sarcophagus with spikes on the inner surfaces. Once the victim was inside, the doors were closed. There, the strategically placed spikes would pierce several vital organs. The wounds wouldn't be instantly fatal. Instead, the victim would linger and bleed to death over several hours.

In June 1899 a poster produced by the *Yorkshire Herald* promoted what promised to be a bizarre and (for most people) disturbing series of lectures every afternoon at 3.00pm and evening at 8.00pm:

> *A series of lectures upon object lessons, consisting of actual instruments of torture now sanctioned by the Roman Church used by the Romanizing clergy.*

Exhibits included a 'Spiked Iron Cage from the Kilburn Sisterhood, used for the Incarceration of Children in their Orphanages; Hair Shirts, Rope, Steel Whips, Armlets, steel with sharp points, Cinctures'.

Admission was free; questions were invited; lectures were given by members of the Protestant Alliance.

93

The Merchant Adventurer's Hall

One of the finest mediaeval guild halls in the world

The Merchant Adventurers' Hall – the resplendent coat of arms.

In Fossgate, this fine building was built on the site of the original 1357 building in 1667; the 15th-century Great Hall and Chapel of Holy Trinity still survive, as do Mercer's records going back to the early 14th century. These provide us with a wealth of information on trade in

York at the time. The hall is one of York's four surviving guildhalls for the 50 or so mercantile and craft guilds here; the others are the Guildhall, Merchant Taylor's in Aldwark, and St Anthony's Hall in Peaseholme Green. Typically for guildhalls, it had two mutual functions: the secular trade side and the religious guild (originally The Fraternal and Guild of Our Lord and the Blessed Virgin, assuming its current name in 1581) to which commercial profits were channelled to justify the business activity and to finance the hospital which was in the Undercroft. The French motto is 'God give us good (business) ventures'. It was made in about 1850 by MN Hassey, who also carved the bust of Shakespeare at the York Theatre Royal and a statue of the Virgin Mary at the Bar Convent. The company used the coat of arms of the Merchant Adventurers of England until 1969, when they were granted their own. The lower part of the hall is built mainly of brick – the earliest surviving made in York after the Romans.

The Company of Merchant Adventurers of the City of York

A Merchant Adventurer was a merchant who risked his own money in pursuit of his trade or craft. For centuries, up until 1835 when the Municipal Corporations Act transferred control to local councils, the Guilds were all- powerful and controlled York's trade and industry. To do business in the city, it was necessary to be elected a Freeman of the City: a man or a woman had to be a Freeman before membership was allowed to the craft guilds.

The Merchant Adventurers Guild goes back to 1357 when a number of prominent York men and women joined together to form a religious fraternity and to build the Merchant Adventurers' Hall. By 1430 most members were merchants of one kind or another; they then set up a trading association or guild using the Great Hall to conduct their business affairs and to meet socially, to look after the poor in the almshouses in the Undercroft and to worship in the Chapel.

See:

Historic England. 'Merchant Taylors' Hall (1259571)', *National Heritage List for England.*

Merchant Adventurers of York, *The York Mercers and Merchant Adventurers, 1356-1917*, Legare Street Press, 2022.

Hartshorne, Pam, *The York Merchant Adventurers and their Hall*, Third Millennium, 2011.

94

The Guildhall

'One of the city's most significant heritage assets'

The Guildhall is situated on the River Ouse behind The Mansion House. It was built in 1445 on the site of the earlier 'Common Hall', dating from at least 1256, and was originally for the Guild of St Christopher and St George and the Corporation, who took over completely in 1549. Council meetings are still held there in the Victorian Council Chamber of 1891. It was used as a theatre – Richard III watched Credo here in 1483 – and as a Court of Justice, and was where Margaret Clitherow was tried in 1586.

In 1647, during the Civil War, Cromwell agreed to pay a ransom of £200,000 to the Scots in exchange for Charles I; the money was counted here. It contains a bell captured at the Siege of Rangoon in 1851. The Guildhall was badly damaged in the Baedeker Raid of 1942, but after the war it was rebuilt and a new stained-glass window, depicting five aspects of the city's history (architecture, war, civic affairs, commercial trade and religious education), was designed and installed by Harry Harvey of York. The subterranean Common Hall Lane passes under the Guildhall – then called Common Hall, to a jetty on the river, originally a continuation of Stonegate.

In 2002 the Guildhall was magnificently renovated. Its latest incarnation offers opportunities to help business start-ups. It is now a 'world-class venue that supports and nurtures the expansion of York's vibrant businesses, combining events and exhibition space with state-of-the-art collaboration and co-working facilities in the heart of a historic and creative city. In Autumn 2017, when restoration work began at the Guildhall, temporary arrangements were put in place for the council to meet in the former Salvation Army Citadel on Gillygate. The renovation, which cost £21 million and was carried out to remedy serious structural issues, was completed in 2022 and the building was subsequently leased to the University of York, as a centre for start up businesses.

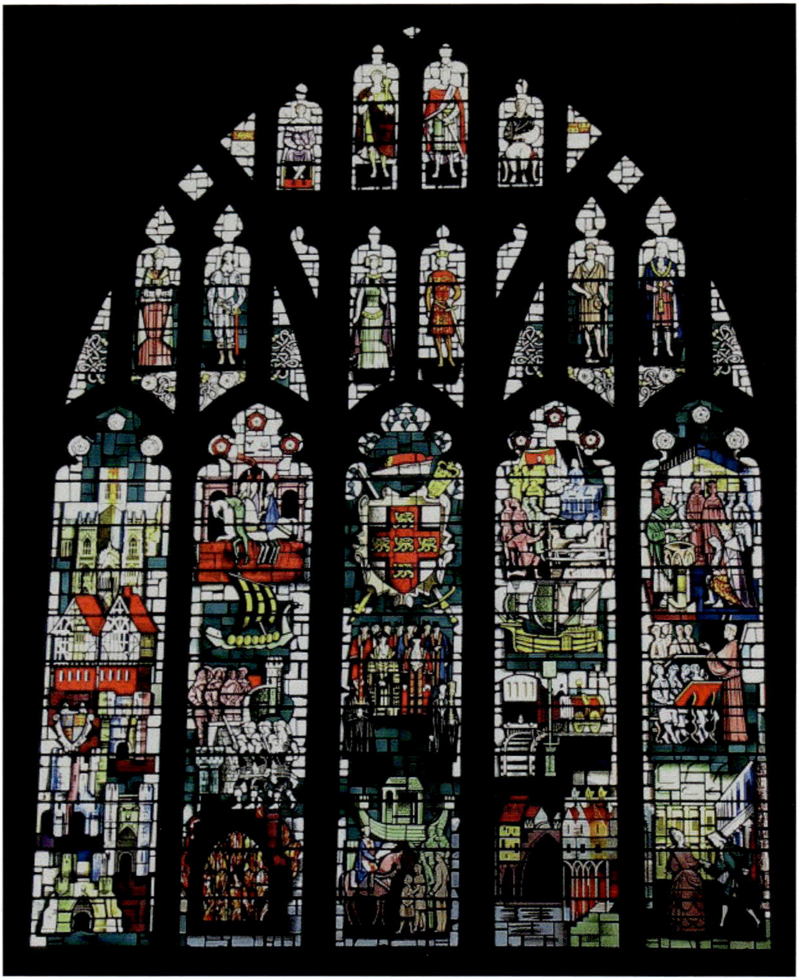

One of the magnificent windows in the Guildhall, depicting much overseas trading.

See:

'York Guildhall Painted Glass Window', History of York.

95

Ivar the Boneless

He wasn't really boneless, just chubby

A depiction of Ívarr and Ubba setting forth to avenge their father, Loðbrók, as it appears on folio 47v of British Library Harley 2278 (15th century).

Ivar was boneless on account of his chubby face, not because he was some kind of medical miracle. Some of the sagas describe him as lacking legs/bones or having a skeletal condition such as osteogenesis imperfecta, while a passage in *Ragnarssona þáttr (The Tale of Ragnar's Sons)* has it that his bonelessness indicates erectile dysfunction. Not good for a rapacious Viking.

The son of Ragnar Lothbrok, in 865 Ivar, with his brother Halfdan Ragnarsson (Halfdene), led the Great Heathen Army and took East Anglia. The following year, on 1 November, they captured York. The date was no coincidence, it being All Saints Day when much of the population would have been preoccupied in the old cathedral, or drunk.

Legend has it that Ivar was fair, big, strong, and one of the wisest men who has ever lived. Ivar was a legendary berserker – Norse warriors who in Old Norse literature are reported to have fought in a frenzied, trance-like fury (from which our word berserk is derived). Berserkers worked themselves into a rage before battle, possibly helped by drugged foods.

Sweyn Forkbeard (d. 1040)

The King of Norway, Denmark and England in 1013-4, father of King Canute, is buried in York.

See:

'Saga of Ivar (The Boneless) Ragnarsson | Up Helly Aa', www.uphellyaa.org.

Groeneveld, Emma, *'Ivar the Boneless,, World History Encyclopedia.*

96

The Porch of St Wilfrid's

'One of the most perfectly finished Catholic Churches in England'

The magnificant doorway.

St Wilfrid and his church have been associated with this site since before the Norman Conquest. Catholics call today's Gothic Revival church the 'Mother Church of the city of York.' The arch over the main door has the most detailed Victorian carving to be seen in the city. The church you see now was completed in 1864; it is replete with sculptures, paintings and stained glass. It is currently part of the Roman Catholic Diocese of Middlesbrough and was the second pro-Cathedral of the Diocese of Beverley until its Dissolution in 1878.

97

York in so Many Words…

The city of York is one of the most important, and popular, cities in the United Kingdom; it always has been, since Roman and Viking times, and it has enjoyed its occasional status as our second city throughout British history. Our Kings and Queens visited often, Parliament sat here, the Royal Mint minted our money here, the Council of the North assembled here while the Pilgrimage of Grace started here. The Archbishop of York is, of course, second only to the Archbishop of Canterbury, while the glorious Minster is the biggest cathedral north of Milan. No wonder then that, throughout history, York has been on the lips of some of the country's most celebrated and influential people. Here are just some of them…

Alcuin (c 732–804)

From the introduction to his *On the Saints of the Church of York*:

> *… My heart is set to praise my home And briefly tell the ancient cradling Of York's famed city through the charms of verse …*

***Domesday* York (1086)**

York's entry tells us about the 1,418 houses in 1086 with such detail as 'Odo the Crossbowman has three dwellings, of Forne and Orne… Landric the carpenter has ten and half dwellings which the sheriff assigned to him'.

William of Malmesbury

Writing in 1125, the father of British history shows us how little has really changed in 900 years with regard to the north-south divide debate:

> *Next in rank after Canterbury is York… almost everything about the language of the North, and particularly of the people of York, is so crude and discordant that we southerners cannot understand it. This is because they are near to barbarian peoples* [the Scots] *and far from the English kings.*

Edward III

Edward III married Philippa of Hainault in the Minster; he was not impressed, as this letter of 1332 makes clear: '... detesting the abominable smell abounding in the said city more than in any other city in the realm from dung and manure and other filth and dirt.' He goes on to order the mayor to clean up the city.

John Leland

Visited York in 1534 and gave a very detailed account; this is typical:

> *And thens over Fosse by a bridge to the castel. Fosse bridge of [5] arches above it; Laithorpbridge on Fosse of 3 arches. Monke bridge on Fosse of 5 arches without Goodrome gate.*

The Abbot of York to Oliver Cromwell, 1556, Rolls House MS.

There be such a company of wilful gentlemen within Yorkshire as there be not in all England besides.

William Camden

In 1586 Camden wrote in his Latin *Britannia*, the first guide book to Britain:

> *York is the second city of England, the most beautiful of this region and indeed the whole north, as well as its principal fortress. It is pleasant, large, and strongly fortified, adorned with private as well as public buildings, crammed with riches and with people ...*

William Shakespeare (1564–1616)

Heads and quarters of traitors were routinely displayed on the top of Micklegate Bar, most famously Richard Duke of York after the Battle of Wakefield in 1460.. The opening lines of *Richard III* refer to '*the sun of York*', a punning reference to the sun badge of Edward IV. Ann Vavasour was the mysterious 'dark' lady of Shakespeare's *Sonnets.*

James Ryther

Ryther here reports back to Lord Burghley, chief advisor to Elizabeth I. Ryther was a fan of neither the people of York, nor of the city itself. He remarked on a strange infatuation with the place of cows in York society and was particularly disappointed by the local beer and the stinginess of York people:

> *Their usury... is more than Jewish... for all their use of drinking inordinately, yet [there is] no faculty as a common brewer in their city by which their beer is not good or wholesome. Their ale is mingled with resin to make it strong, in some parts with urine... the magistrates are so simple.*

Richard Norwood

Norwood, a 'reader in the Mathematicks' published his *A Sea-Mans Practice* in 1637, detailing the painstaking journey he made, on foot, from London to 'the Cittye of Yorke'. It took him two years, and, not one for travelling light, carried with him a 90ft chain, a 5ft sextant and a magnetic compass. His aim? To determine accurately the 'distance occupied by one degree along a great circle of the Earth'. Assuming he took Sundays off, he would have covered 1,700 feet per day, making 10,300 measurements with his chain. Ever since Ptolemy in AD 100, the accepted distance for one degree was 60 miles; after Norwood it was extended by 16 per cent. Norwood had a significant influence on Sir Isaac Newton's *Philisophiae Naturalis Principia Mathematica* of 1686. Norwood's book was reprinted five times.

Celia Fiennes

The intrepid lady traveller journeyed the length and breadth of the country, often with only one or two maids in attendance; she visited York in 1697. This is how she described the River 'Ouise' and the mean streets of York in her journal *Great Journey to Newcastle and to Cornwall*:

> *It bears Great Barges, it Looks muddy, its full of good ffish. We Eate very good Cod fish and Salmon and that at a pretty Cheape rate, tho' we were not in the best jnn for the Angel is the best in Cunny Streete. The houses are very Low and as indifferent as in any Country town and the Narrowness of y^e Streetes makes it appear very mean.*

Celia Fiennes, typically on horseback.

Francis Drake (not that one)

Drake (1696–1771) was an eminent York surgeon at York County Hospital and author of the landmark *Eboracum, or the History and Antiquities of the City of York.* Some things have changed, some have not, as this extract shows:

> *Our streets are kept clean, and lighted with lamps, every night in the winter season; and so regular are the inhabitants, to their hours of rest, that it is rare to meet any person, after ten or eleven at night… the common people are very well made and proportioned… the women are remarkably handsome; it being taken notice of by strangers that they observe more pretty faces in York than in any other place… the better sort talk the English language in perfection at York. Without the affected tone and mincing speech of the southern people.*

He became a member of the Royal Society; debts landed Drake in a debtor's prison until bailed out by his patron.

Daniel Defoe

There is abundance of good company here, and abundance of good families live here, for the sake of the good company and cheap living; a man converses here with all the world as effectually as at London.

This is how Daniel Defoe generously described York in his *A Tour Thro' The Whole Island Of Great Britain*, from 1724. He described Ouse Bridge 'near 70 foot in diameter; it is, without exception, the greatest in England, some say it's as large as the Rialto at Venice, though I think not.' With the distinct advantage of seeing things from the outside, Defoe liked the prison, describing it as 'the most stately and complete of any in the whole kingdom, if not in Europe'. Defoe's Robinson Crusoe opens with 'I was born in the year 1862, in the city of York, of a good family ...'

Laurence Sterne

Sterne (1713–1768) is famous for his *The Life and Opinions of Tristram Shandy, Gentleman*, and *A Sentimental Journey Through France and Italy*; he was also an Anglican clergyman with a vicarship at nearby Sutton-on-the-Forest, a living at Stillington and a prebendary of York Minster, lodging at Hildyard's in Stonegate**.** Sterne married Elizabeth Lumley, who lived in College Street. His satire *A Political Romance* (1759), exposed political infighting at the Minster. Sterne died of pleurisy in London in 1768; he is buried in the churchyard in Coxwold, but only after a circuitous journey… having been originally interred in St George's churchyard, Hanover Square, London. His body was snatched by 'resurrection men' for use in medical dissection at Cambridge University. The cadaver was recognised by the Professor of Anatomy there, who fainted when he saw it on the table and had it hastily reburied. In 1969 the Lawrence Sterne Society obtained permission to remove Sterne's remains to Coxwold for re-burial. Dr John Burton was the model for Dr Slop in *Tristram Shandy*; he once lived in the Red House in York; Burton was a gynaecologist and medical author whose books included *An Essay Towards a Complete System of Midwifery.*

Tobias Smollett

The Expedition of Humphry Clinker published in 1771, features York's Assembly Rooms: somewhere sumptuous where the local gentry could play dice and cards, dance and take tea. Smollett was not impressed: 'the company, on a ball night, must look like an assembly of fantastic fairies, revelling by moonlight among the columns of a Grecian temple'. In his *Travels* – letters sent home from Boulogne, Paris, Nice, and other places – he saw in Durham Cathedral and York Minster 'gloomy and depressing piles'.

William Alexander and Scott's Dr Dryasdust

One of York's earliest booksellers and printers, Alexander refused to publish secular novels, considering them far too ephemeral. His self-censorship was to cost him dear. Walter Scott (1771–1832), while researching *Ivanhoe,* came to York and visited Alexander's bookshop, where he suggested Alexander might publish his book. Alexander declined, saying 'I esteem your friendship but I fear thy books are too worldly for me to print'. He paid for his rebuff, though, as the bookseller is thought to be reborn as the boring Dr Dryasdust to whom Scott dedicated *Ivanhoe.* Castlegate provides the setting for Walter Scott's *The Severn Stars,* where Jeanie Deans stayed en route to London in *Heart of Midlothian.*

The Cries of York

York, like other cities, had its own repertoire of cries. Some of these were compiled in a penny book and published by J Kendrew of Colliergate in 1811 'for the amusement of good children'. Typical are:

> *Threepence a quart, Ripe Goosberries, Ripe gooseberries at York you'll buy, As cheap as cheap can be, Of many sorts you hear the cry, Pray purchase sir of me'* and *'A list of horses that's to start On Knavesmire, and each name; With riders that are dressed so smart, Anxious the prize to claim.*

Sydney Smith (1771–1845)

The streets of York required some skill in this art [coach driving]. My father once exclaiming to one of the principal tradesmen there 'why, Mr Brown, your streets are the narrowest in Europe'.

Charles Dickens

On one of his visits to York in 1838, Dickens describes in his *Letters* a visit to his friend, John Camidge, organist at the Minster, who showed him round. Dickens was particularly struck by 'the deep organ's bursting heart throb through the shivering air' and the Five Sisters Window. Dickens's story about the window appears in *Nicholas Nickleby* as the *Five Sisters of York*. The first reading was given in York at the long-gone Festival Concert Rooms in Blake Street; the *Yorkshire Gazette* tells us that Dickens 'elicited unbounded applause and sent his audience home delighted'. Mr Micawber from *David Copperfield*, too, finds his origins in York, based as he is on a Richard Chicken, a feckless character who in 1847 worked in the same railway office as Albert Dickens, Charles's railway engineer brother. Chicken was also an actor and at one time a self-styled Professor of Elocution and Lecturer on Defective Annunciation.

Wilkie Collins (1824–89)

A frequent visitor, he set his 1862 novel, *No Name*, in the city describing a walk along the walls by Captain Wragge as:

> *One of the most striking scenes which England can show… the majestic west front of York Minster soared over the city and caught the last brightest light of heaven on the summits of its lofty towers.*

On the other hand, his description of Skeldergate is less uplifting: 'dingy warehouses and joyless private residences of red brick'.

Elizabeth Gaskell

The Mansion House is famously threatened with being burnt to the ground in Gaskell's *Sylvia's Lovers* (1863) if the Mayor, in 1777, failed to satisfy the demands of the press-gang.

The Impress Service arrived in York on 18 January 1777 'to beat up for volunteers'. So angry were sections of the community that a letter was soon sent to the Lord Mayor threatening to burn down the Mansion House if the gang was not expelled. A reward of 100 guineas was offered for conviction of the author or authors of the missive and a 12-man guard was put on the Mansion House. Some ill-disposed citizens used the presence of the press gang as an opportunity for revenge: to rid themselves of enemies by reporting scandalous and incriminating stories to the lieutenant; or to benefit financially by posing as the press gang, seizing men and extorting money from their families for release. The real gang departed on 14 February 'having picked up a great number of hands for His Majesty's Service', as reported in the *York Courant*.

WH Auden

Wystan Hugh Auden was born at number 54, Bootham, on 21 February 1907; his father, GA Auden, was Medical Officer for York and author of *The Gild of Barber Surgeons of the City of York.*

JB Priestley

In 1933 Priestley wrote in his *English Journey:* 'York is, of course, the guide-book man's paradise, and not without good reason, for if you want the past, here it is, weighing tons.'

Margaret C. Barnet, *The Barber Surgeons of York* (1968)

Of the two views you can take of mediaeval York, perhaps the most popular is that of a great and important city, the capital of the North, the base for operations against the Scots, the seat of the Archbishop; a town owing much to the prosperity of the wool trade, to which ships came from all over Europe. It was a beautiful place, with the towers and spires of the many ecclesiastical buildings new and bright in the clear light. In addition to the Minster, there were St Mary's Abbey, monasteries, friaries, 40 churches, and the walls and bars which were kept in good repair... all combine to make a cheerful picture.

But there is another view of York and it is an equally true one. It is of the city at times when trade was bad, when there was much unemployment, or at times of great and recurring epidemics. York in the middle ages was a death trap. Deaths always exceeded births. It was a notoriously dirty and smelly place. In fact, one king said it was the worst in his kingdom. A royal visit was often a blessing since the council would attempt a thorough cleansing and banish the pigs – those inefficient and inadequate scavengers from the streets. There were no drains, usually only a central gutter in the street down which water and refuse were expected to flow. Whilst it was forbidden to throw rubbish into the Ouse, the number of references to fines imposed make it obvious that it was the common receptacle for what was described as 'nastiness'. Nightsoil and manure were put outside the houses and then carted away to recognised sites such as Toft Green to be sold later by manure merchants to the farmers. Behind the houses in closes and yards there were often stables and sheds for the cattle brought in from the strays.

Donald Gray, Headmaster, Bootham School

When the Quaker Bootham School was evacuated to Roman Catholic and rural Ampleforth during World War Two, Donald Gray, the head at the time, is reputed to have addressed the combined school as 'Friends, Romans and Countrymen'.

98

George Stubbs and Dr Slop

'A little squat, uncourtly figure ... about four feet and a half perpendicular height, with a breadth of back, and a sesquipedality of belly'

Dr Slop, with his wig on fire, angrily gesticulating to Susannah, who holds her nose near the wounded baby (Wellcome Collection).

The present Hull-York Medical School is York's second medical school. The first was founded in 1834, encouraged by members of York Medical Society. Unfortunately, it was short lived and closed in 1858, but not before it had attracted renowned teachers like George Stubbs (anatomist and later horse painter).

Dr Slop is an irritable physician and ' in Laurence Sterne's picaresque novel *The Life and Opinions of Tristram Shandy, Gentleman* (1759). Sterne paints him unflatteringly as 'a little squat, uncourtly figure ... about four feet and a half perpendicular height, with a breadth of back, and a sesquipedality of belly'.

John Burton (1710-1771) obstetrician and Laurence Sterne's Dr Slop; Burton was also a man midwife and medical author whose books included *An Essay Towards a Complete System of Midwifery*, illustrated by no less an artist than George Stubbs. In 1738 he moved to York where, in 1740, he was one of the forces behind the founding of the York Hospital, becoming its first physician.

Burton was also a capable classical scholar and an eminent antiquarian. In 1758 he published the *Monasticou Eboraceuse and ecclesiastical history of Yorkshire*, an important contribution to the archaeology of the county; further tracts on Yorkshire antiquities followed in 1768–71. He died on 19 January 1771, and was buried in Holy Trinity Church, Micklegate. His wife, Mary, was buried at his side a few months later.

Then there was **John Hughlings Jackson** (d. 1911), neurologist and house physician to the York Dispensary, best known for his work on epilepsy – the new medical school building bears his name. **Daniel Hack Tuke** (d. 1895, great grandson of William Tuke), a psychiatrist who trained at the Retreat and in 1853 visited a number of foreign asylums, and later back in York he was appointed visiting physician to the York Retreat and the York Dispensary, lecturing also to the York School of Medicine on mental diseases. **James Atkinson** (d. 1839) was a surgeon, friend of Sterne and author of *Medical Bibliography A&B* , the dedication in which reads: 'To all idle medical students in Great Britain'. A rare and eccentric humorous work, *Obstetric Ejaculations on Cow Pock* (apparently privately printed in 1808), is attributed to Atkinson. He died at the age of 80 at Lendal, on 14 March 1839. He was buried at St Helen's, Stonegate. His brother was the doctor **Charles Atkinson**, who wrote the 'rural poem' *Neighbourhood of Heslington*, dedicated to Henry Yarburgh of Heslington Hall.

Stubbs had come to York (then, as now, a centre of excellence in medical science) to learn his anatomy. Stubbs found work teaching medical students in the Medical School before taking up comparative anatomy, and painting his famous horses. His most celebrated, *Whistlejacket*, was painted in 1762 and featured the very same horse that won the four-mile chase for 2,000 guineas at York's Knavesmire in August 1759.

See:

Burton J, *An essay towards a complete new system of midwifery, etc.,* London, 1751.

Dunn PM, 'Dr John Burton (1710–1771) of York and his obstetric treatise', *Archives of Disease in Childhood – Fetal and Neonatal Edition* 2001; 84: F74-F76.

Rogers, Deborah D, 'Eighteenth-Century Literary Depictions of Childbirth in the Historical Context of Mutilation And Mortality: The Case of "Pamela"." *The Centennial Review*, vol. 37, no. 2, 1993, pp. 305–24.

99

The Yorkshire Museum

The Yorkshire Museum was founded by the Yorkshire Philosophical Society to display their geological and archaeological collections. It was originally in Ousegate until 1828 when the society received, by royal grant, ten acres of land from St Mary's Abbey in order to build a new museum in what is now Museum Gardens. The main building was designed by William Wilkins in Greek Revival style; it was officially opened in 1830, making it one of the oldest museums in Britain. A condition of the royal grant was that the surrounding land should become a botanical garden. This was completed in the 1830s.

The biology collection contains 200,000 specimens, geology has over 112,500 specimens; the archaeology collection has nearly a million objects dating from around 500,000 BCE to the 20th century and includes the York Helmet (750-775), discovered in York in 1982. In 1992 the Museum paid £2.5 million for the Middleham Jewel.

Recent exhibitions have included, from the website:

Yorkshire's Jurassic World

Mediaeval York: Capital of the North

Visit 'Mediaeval York: Capital of the North' and explore how York became England's second city and how its fortunes rose and fell with its ties to Crown and the Church.

A display showcasing a range of fantastic archaeological material and scientific specimens which tell the story of Yorkshire from its beginnings to the arrival of the Romans.

Ritual or Disguise: The Star Carr Headdresses

Features four Mesolithic headdresses discovered at the archaeological site in Star Carr, which have never seen in public before together, along with new research by the team at the University of York.

The Four Seasons mosaic (courtesy of York Museum Trust).

Roman York – Meet the People of the Empire

One of the best collections in Britain, as befits a prominent Roman city. Discover what life was like before, during and after the Roman invasion of York. Explore fascinating finds including sculptures and carvings, ceramics and tools, through to skeletons and burial items, and a stunning mosaic floor.

Highlights include:

William Smith: the map that changed the world

Discover a map that literally changed the way the world thought about what was beneath its feet. Measuring 1.8m by 2.6m, William 'Strata' Smith's map went on to inspire scientists to work out a more accurate age of the planet.

Prehistoric

- The Star Carr Pendant, the oldest Mesolithic art in Britain.

Roman

- The Wold Newton hoard, a hoard of 1,857 coins dating from the early fourth century AD.
- The Head of Constantine the Great, a fragment of a marble statue of the Roman Emperor Constantine the Great.
- The Statue of Mars, a fourth-century sculpture of the Roman god Mars.
- The Heslington Hoard, a hoard of 2,800 coins dating from the mid-fourth century AD.
- The Ivory Bangle Lady, a fourth-century skeleton of a woman.
- The Ryedale Hoard contains some of Yorkshire's most significant Roman objects, including an 1,800-year-old bust of Marcus Aurelius. The 13cm bust is part of a collection of bronze objects found by metal detectorists James Spark and Mark Didlick in a field near Ampleforth, North Yorkshire, in May 2020.

The Ryedale Hoard (courtesy of York Museum Trust).

Early Mediaeval

- The Coppergate Helmet, an eighth-century helmet found in York.
- The Ormside Bowl, a silver-gilt bowl from Cumbria.
- A portion of the St Leonard's Place hoard of ninth-century Northumbrian pennies.
- The Bedale Hoard, a hoard of Viking silver jewellery and an Anglo-Saxon sword.
- The Gilling sword, a late Anglo-Saxon sword found in a river.

The Coppergate Helmet (courtesy of York Museum Trust).

Mediaeval

- The Middleham Jewel, a gold, diamond-shaped pendant set with a sapphire and engraved with a picture of the Christian Trinity on the front, and one of the Nativity of Jesus on the back.
- The Ryther Hoard
- The mediaeval shrines of Saint William of York.
- A gilt-enamel figurine depicting Christ, produced in Limoges enamel, which was discovered in 1826 and subsequently lost, was purchased by the Museum in 2019. It first went on public display on 20 September 2019.

The Middleham Jewel (courtesy of York Museum Trust).

Courtesy of York Museum Trust.

Courtesy of York Museum Trust.

Fragment of Legio IX Hispana Tablet

Inscription with well-formed Roman letters and numbers. Described in *Eboracum* as:

> *Commemorative Tablet fragment in magnesian limestone, comprising the middle part, 3 and 1/3 ft by 3 and 3/4 ft, of an inscription recording the building in stone of the SE gate of the fortress under Trajan. The fine lettering decreases in height from 6 ins in the first line to 3 and 1/2 ins in the last. Found in 1854 at a depth of 26ft to 28ft in King's Square near the house at the corner of Goodramgate and King's Square in making a drain along Goodramgate and Church Street.*

Hair piece, found in a sarcophagus containing a lead coffin and gypsum. The lead coffin was decorated with a corded pattern. The preservation of the hair is really very unusual – presumably it had been treated with something prior to interment that has affected it in this way. The head may have originally laid upon a pillow, preventing initial contact with the gypsum. Two cantharus-headed jet pins remain in situ in the hair.

Canon Raine (YPS Proceedings 1875):

> *In this place was found a long folded tress , the back hair, in fact, of a young Roman lady. It might almost have been combed when it was first discovered, it was so limp. Fixed in it are two beautifully wrought pins of jet. By the side of what had once been the cheeks, and in the fragments of the skull, were other small portions of hair which have been preserved. The bones of the skull and body were all in pieces; very little remained of the body or its garniture, save this beautiful curl.*

Courtesy of York Museum Trust.

100

The Six Bars of York and a Postern

In the city where bars are gates and gates are streets and alleys are snickelways.

Bootham Bar (courtesy of the York Press, published in the York Press, 22 October 2018, this was their caption:

We don't know who the anonymous artist was who painted the 1800 watercolour of Bootham Bar which we start off with here. But we have a lot to thank him for.

He painted the bar at a time when it still had its barbican, for one thing. And he also captured some long-vanished buildings that used to lean up against the bar – some of them with beautifully carved details around the windows.

Look at the painting long enough, however, and you might begin to think you're seeing things. It was painted from outside the bar, looking through the arch towards Petergate, with the Minster looming behind. But isn't the cathedral in the wrong place?)

Bootham Bar

'Not fit for any female of respectability to pass'

Bootham Bar (originally Buthum, which means at the booths and signifies the markets which used to be held here) stands on the north-western gateway of the Roman fortress and was originally called Galmanlith. A door knocker was added to the Bar in 1501 for the use of Scotsmen (and others presumably) seeking admission to the city. The barbican came down in 1831 and the wall steps went up in 1889; a statue of Ebrauk, the pre-Roman founder of York, once stood nearby. Thomas Mowbray's severed head was stuck here in 1405 and the Earl of Manchester bombarded the Bar in 1644 during the Civil war. The barbican was removed in 1831. The removal of the barbican was due in part to complaints by residents of Clifton: 'not fit for any female of respectability to pass through' on account of the droppings of animals en route to the cattle market and its use as a urinal by pedestrians. The three statues on the top were carved in 1894 and feature a mediaeval mayor, a mason and a knight; the mason is holding a model of the restored Bar.

Fishergate Bar

Sometimes called St George's Bar, this is the gateway to Selby; chains ran across the River Foss here to the castle to reinforce York's defences near the wall-less swamp that was the King's Fishpond. In Elizabethan times it was a prison for rascals and lunatics.

'Barram Fishergate' is the first documented reference to the bar, in 1315. A central stone above the archway reveals the date of the current bar and features the York coat of arms and an inscription which reads:

'A.doi m.cccc.lxxx.vii Sr Willm Tod knight mayre this wal was mayd in his days lx yadys'

This reveals that 60 yards of the wall, including the bar, was built in 1487 under Sir William Tod, Mayor of York.

But just two years later, in 1489, Fishergate Bar suffered considerable damage in the Yorkshire Peasants' Revolt against the tax burden imposed by Henry VII following the murder of Henry Percy, 4th Earl of Northumberland. Henry Percy had betrayed King Richard III at the battle of Bosworth Field by remaining inactive and submitting to Henry after the battle. Richard had been popular in York, but four years previously the city had expressed its 'great heaviness' at his death.

The Earl came to deliver the King's demand and collect the taxes; however, on the 28 April 1489, at a meeting he had arranged with the citizens to discuss their grievances about the taxes, an angry mob, led by a man called Chambre, claimed that Henry's predecessor, Richard III, would never have allowed his people to be oppressed by such a heavy tax, and that the Earl was a 'scurvy rogue'.

The mob of deeply angered citizens attacked the earl, who was then 'furiously and shamefully murdered and killed'. Soon after this the revolt was supressed and the gateway was bricked up and was not re-opened until 1834, to give better access for the cattle market.

Fishergate Bar.

The King's Fishpool – '*the disgrace of York... a stinking morass*'

Stagnating around the Red Tower, created when the Normans dammed the River Foss. It was variously described as 'the disgrace of York...a stinking morass' and by Francis Drake as the repository for 'any dung of beasts or other nastinesses'. The Corporation drained it in 1854 and built Foss Islands Road.

Monk Bar

Built around 1330 it was originally called Monkgate Bar; at 63ft it is the tallest of York's Bars. Designed as a self-contained fortress, assailants had to cross each floor to reach the next flight of stairs, thus exposing themselves to defensive fire. A perfect fortress, the Bar features loopholes (for bows and arrows); gun ports and murder holes from which heavy objects and boiling water might be dropped. The coat of arms is Plantagenet. The Bar was used as a prison in the 16th century for recusant Catholics, and others: in 1588 Robert Walls was imprisoned for 'drawing blood in a fray'. The barbican was removed in the early 1800s. To rent the rooms at the top, one Thomas Pak (Master Mason at the Minster) paid 4s per annum.

Monk Bar.

Victoria Bar

This bar was built in 1838 and named after the new Queen. It gave access to the city in the Nunnery Lane/Bishophill area. The gate consists of a central archway with two flanking pedestrian arches. The two additional arches were created in 1864 and 1867. During construction an earlier archway was uncovered, which showed signs of having been hastily blocked up. This was probably the 12th century Bar known as Lounelith, or 'secluded gate'; the blockade was possibly part of the strengthening of the city's defences in the Northern Rebellion in 1569.

Walmgate Bar

Walmgate Bar comprises a three-storey gatehouse and a single-storey barbican; the barbican creates a long, exposed narrow passage which attackers would have been forced to cross before reaching the portcullis and heavy oak doors. The design was state-of-the-art in the 14th century, but it was unable to withstand Parliamentary cannon in the Civil War Siege of York. The Bar was originally known as Walbesgate and is the only York Bar with its barbican (14th century), portcullis and 15th-century inner oak doors intact, thanks largely to William Etty RA who campaigned tirelessly for its preservation. Indeed, Walmgate Bar is the only town gate in England to survive with its barbican intact.

In 1489, during the Yorkshire Rebellion, it was set on fire by rebels; the rebels met with the Earl of Northumberland, but the meeting descended into violence and the Earl was killed. Henry VII's response was to send an army to York – the rebellion evaporated but not before Walmgate Bar was set on fire and badly damaged. The inner facade is 16th century and still retains its Doric and Ionic columns. At its rear is a small timber-framed building, which was leased as a house; in 1376 an annual rent of 10 shillings was paid. The artist and historian, John Browne, was born here in 1793.

The most significant repairs to Walmgate Bar were made in 1648 after undergoing severe cannon shot damage during the Siege of York in the Civil War, and again in 1840 after years of dilapidation. Cannon from Lamel Hill and St Lawrence churchyard bombarded the Bar and Parliamentary soldiers mined the approach to the gateway. The mine tunnel was filled in 1645. The Corporation of York couldn't afford to repair the Bar but Parliament granted £5,000 for the work in 1648.

Fishergate Postern

The Fishergate Postern Tower, one of six original postern towers on the walls, marks the end of the mediaeval walls in the section to the east of the Foss that runs from the Red Tower. The present tower is the second postern tower to occupy the site.

The original tower was the Talken Tower, named after Robert de Talken, a wine merchant, who was York's mayor in 1399. The present tower was built between 1504 and 1507, with the exception of the tiled roof, which was added in the 16th century. The Postern itself is a small entrance with a pointed archway, the only surviving one of its type left in York. There is a groove inside which once held a portcullis.

The later three-storey Fishergate Postern *posternam iuxta Skarletpit* dates from 1502 and is York's only surviving example. Buildings adjoining the postern were destroyed in a 1489 riot. The tower was originally called Edward's tower. A projecting lavatory discharged into the adjacent King's Pool.

Dick Turpin's grave is nearby in the garden on the site of St George's Church. He was executed on 7 April 1739 after spending time in a cell which can still be seen in the Debtor's Prison in the Castle Museum.

101

The Joseph Rowntree Statue

No, not a mistake: there is, of course, still no statue in York celebrating the life and countless achievements of this enlightened and philanthropic man.

Incredible as it seems, successive councils have never been moved to honour Rowntree in such a fitting, visible and dignified way. York makes much of Dick Turpin, armed robber, and of Guido Fawkes, anarchist conspirator and would-be mass murderer. York celebrates George Leeman with a prominent statue despite him being a bit of an afterthought and York is perennially ambivalent about the 'railway king', George Hudson.

But, blue plaque and birthplace black plaque apart, York has consistently failed to appropriately honour Joseph Rowntree, he who brought unimaginable prosperity to the city and to many of its workers from which York citizens and pensioners still benefit to this day, he who put York on the business map of the world by founding one of the most successful confectionery companies ever, he who bequeathed two schools, a theatre, a company library, a 30-acre expansive park complete with gates, a swimming pool, and an entire village with model garden, village housing, fresh air and social facilities in a time of industrial pollution and back-to-back slummery, he who established a pioneering works pension scheme, leading the way with other enlightened workplace benefits.

What on earth do you have to do to get a modest statue erected in gratitude for all that he has done and for his prodigious legacy which continues to benefit the city of York and its people?

Joseph Rowntree (1836-1925), social and charity worker

Here are just some of the less known good causes once supported by Joseph Rowntree in York:

York Anti Slavery Society; York Association for the Prosecution of Felons and Villains; York Society for the Prevention and Discouragement of Vice & Profaneness; Society to Assist the Labouring and Poor Classes of York; the Mission to the Indians; Dr Choke's Society for Promoting Schools in Africa; Society for Promoting Permanent & Universal Peace; Society for Promoting the Education of Native Females in India; the Society for the Prevention of Youthful Depravity; Female Temperance Association; York Society for the Encouragement of Faithful Female Servants; York Meeting Sewing Circle.

A plinth in need of a statue…